PRONGHORN
Hunting

By Toby Bridges &
Don Oster

CREATIVE
PUBLISHING
international

MINNETONKA, MINNESOTA

www.howtobookstore.com

TOBY BRIDGES, an outdoor writer since the late 1960s, has guided for pronghorns for more than 35 years. He's recognized as the country's leading authority on hunting with muzzleloaders. Toby is the author of Creative Publishing's award-winning book, *Muzzleloading*.

DON OSTER has been hunting pronghorns off and on for almost 40 years in Wyoming, Montana and New Mexico. His favorite hunting companion is his son Mark. Their biggest thrill comes from planning and executing a perfect sneak on a good buck. Whoever shoots is immaterial.

President / CEO: David D. Murphy

PRONGHORN HUNTING
By Toby Bridges & Don Oster

Executive Editor, Outdoor Products Group: David R. Maas
Managing Editor: Jill Anderson
Senior Editor: Steven J. Hauge
Copy Editor: Susan Maas
Creative Director: Bradley Springer
Senior Art Director: David W. Schelitzche
Photo Editor and Project Manager: Angela Hartwell
Studio Manager: Marcia Chambers
Studio Photographer: Tate Carlson
Director, Production Services: Kim Gerber
Production Manager: Stasia Dorn
Production Staff: Laura Hokkanen, Helga Thielen, Stephanie Barakos

Cover Photo: Wyman Meinzer

Contributing Photographers: Robert E. Barber, Mike Barlow, George Barnett/Bruce Coleman, Inc., Mike Blair, Toby Bridges, Denver Bryan, Bill Buckley/The Green Agency, Milt Camp, Tim Christie, Michael H. Francis, Patricio Robles Gil/Bruce Coleman, Inc., Donald M. Jones, Mark Kayser, Lee Kline, Bill Lea, Tom & Pat Leeson, Stephen W. Maas, Bill McRae, Wyman Meinzer, Mark Oster, Kennan Ward, Art Wolfe, Gary R. Zahm

Contributing Illustrators: George Catlin (1796-1872), David W. Schelitzche

Contributing Agencies and Manufacturers: Ammo Craft Reloading & Call Pro Shop – Don Parsons; Arizona Game and Fish Department – Richard A. Ockenfels, Duane Shroufe; Boone & Crockett Club – Jack and Susan Reneau, Chris Tonkinson; Bushnell Sports Optics Worldwide – Barbara Mellman; Crooked Horn Outfitters – Lennis Janzen; Double Bull Archery LLC; Irish Setter Sport Boots – Kim Emery; Knives of Alaska – Charles E. Allen; Savage Arms Inc.

Printing: R. R. Donnelley & Sons Co.
10 9 8 7 6 5 4 3 2 1

Library of Congress Cataloging-in-Publication Data

Bridges, Toby.
    Pronghorn hunting / by Toby Bridges.
        p. cm. -- (The complete hunter)
    ISBN 0-86573-157-8
    1. Pronghorn antelope hunting. I. Title. II. Hunting & fishing library. Complete hunter.

SK305.P76 B75 2001
799.2'7639--dc21

                                                    2001028707

Contents

Introduction

Inhabiting the plains and grasslands stretching out along both sides of the great Rocky Mountains, the pronghorn is anything but secretive. Interstate travelers are often treated to the sight of thousands of the animals within a few hundred yards of the highway just about any time of the year. Instead of hiding in brushy creek bottoms or deep draws, the pronghorn seeks the open spaces for protection from its enemies. Sharp eyes and fleet feet are this creature's main lines of defense. Their unequalled ability to spot approaching danger, then quickly flee, once caused early westward adventurers to claim that the pronghorn was impossible to hunt.

Members of the famed Lewis and Clark expedition were among the first white men to lay eyes upon the pronghorn of the American West. In their quest to collect specimens for study, for camp meat, and to send back to Washington D.C. for the national museum, these early muzzleloader hunters discovered just how difficult it was to get within relatively close range of these "antelopes." On September 17, 1804, Meriwether Lewis entered into his journal these observations of the fleet pronghorn:

"I had this day an opportunity of witnessing the agility and the superior fleetness of this animal which was to me really astounding. I had pursued and twice surprised a small herd of seven. In the first instance they did not discover me distinctly and therefore did not run at full speed, though they took care before they rested to gain an elevated point where it was impossible to approach them under cover, except in one direction from which the wind blew toward them. Bad as the chance to approach them was, I made best of my way towards them, frequently peeping over the ridge with which I took care to conceal myself from their view. The male, of which there was but one, frequently encircled the summit of the hill on which the females stood in a group, as if to look out for the approach of danger. I got within about 200 paces of them when they smelled me and fled. I gained the top of the eminence on which they stood, as soon as possible from whence I had extensive view of the country. The antelopes which had disappeared in a steep ravine now appeared at a distance of about three miles on the side of the ridge. So soon had these antelopes gained the distance at which they had again appeared to my view, I doubted at first that they were the same I had just surprised."

Later that day, Lewis wrote, "We found the antelopes extremely shy and watchful in so much that we had been unable to get a shot at them. When at rest they generally select the most elevated point in the neighborhood, and as they are watchful and extremely quick of sight, and their smelling very acute, it is almost impossible to approach them within gunshot."

Hunting the pronghorn hasn't changed all that much in the last 200 years. If anything, the pronghorn has adapted a few tricks of its own to make it even more difficult to hunt than in the past. Even so, the hunter who's willing to spend a few days observing pronghorn movements will discover that this fast-footed speedster of the plains can be very patternable with quite predictable traits, which even make this trophy susceptible to today's hunter who chooses to use a muzzleloader or bow and arrow.

In several western states, hunter success is very high, often topping 80 percent. Finding pronghorns in good habitat normally isn't a problem. In Wyoming, for example, there are nearly as many pronghorns as people. During a hunt in this state, it's rare to glass from an elevated position for an hour without at least seeing pronghorns in the distance. And if you blow a stalk on a good buck, you can very likely be stalking another buck in less than an hour. In most pronghorn country, the hunter with just 3 or 4 days to hunt can usually fill his tag with a decent buck.

A quality, full-shoulder mount of a regal pronghorn buck makes a fine addition to any hunter's den. The nearly black horns, unique facial markings and alternating brown-and-white body patches make the pronghorn one of the most beautifully marked animals in the world. In a room with several deer mounts, a nice 14-inch or better pronghorn mount definitely stands out and is a real attention-getter.

Many hunters consider the fine-grained meat of a pronghorn a real delicacy. When time is taken to quickly skin and cool down the carcass, the pronghorn makes superb tablefare. Some hunters even prefer it over whitetail venison.

So let's see . . . the pronghorn is challenging, plentiful, easy to find, offers multiple opportunities for shots, makes a beautiful mount and provides some tasty tablefare. It definitely has all the qualities for being North America's "perfect" big-game species.

In this book, Don Oster and I take an in-depth look at pronghorn hunting today. By reading the following chapters you'll learn not only about pronghorn behavior, but you'll discover proven hunting tactics for taking a unique trophy animal that was once considered unhuntable.

– Toby Bridges

Understanding
Pronghorns

Pronghorn Basics

From the very beginning the pronghorn has been mistakenly called an antelope. Early observers of this uniquely North American species were quick to associate the animal with the antelopes of Africa. And it's easy to see why. Upon seeing a pronghorn for the first time, the observer witnesses an animal with herd instincts, which is colorful and unusually marked, displays mostly upright, nearly straight horns, is swift and extremely agile, and tends to prefer living out in wide open spaces, much like the antelopes found in Africa. Thus, the name antelope stuck, and to this day more American sportsmen know this plains creature as an antelope instead of by its true name, the pronghorn.

These animals got their name from the flat prong that grows from the main beam of the male antelope's horn. Indigenous only to North America, the one-of-a-kind pronghorn is unique in that it is the only member of a family, genus and species. It has no other living relative in the animal world.

SPECIES. The scientific name of the pronghorn is *Antilocapra americana*, of which many wildlife professionals recognize five different subspecies. The Oregon pronghorn, *Antilocapra americana oregona*, inhabits eastern Oregon. The subspecies known as *Antilocapra americana mexicana* is found on the plains of west Texas, New Mexico and Arizona. The so-called peninsular pronghorn, *Antilocapra americana peninsularis*, makes its home on the Baja Peninsula of Mexico, while the endangered subspecies *Antilocapra americana sonoriensis*, or the Sonora pronghorn, is named after the desert region of northern Mexico where it lives. But of all the subspecies, *Antilocapra americana americana*, simply known as the American pronghorn, is the most widely spread and makes up about 90 percent of the entire North American pronghorn population. The Boone and Crockett Club record book simply recognizes *Antilocapra americana americana* and "related subspecies."

Pronghorn range

Pronghorn doe and buck

PHYSICAL CHARACTERISTICS

SIZE. Hunters often overestimate the size of antelope. This could be due to the relative length of their legs, the lack of trees or sizeable brush in the wide open terrain they inhabit, maybe their light coloration, or perhaps just because there's always 200 or 300 yards between you and them. In any case, when hunters look at a pronghorn from a distance, most guess the animal larger than it really is. Consequently, most hunters have a hard time accurately judging the distance to the animal as well. Most mature bucks weigh between 90 and 140 pounds, the latter being an exceptionally heavy pronghorn. An average buck stands 3 feet at the shoulder and measures approximately 4 to 5 feet in

length. A full-grown doe weighs 10 to 20 percent less than bucks sharing the same range.

COLOR. Very likely the product of millions of years of evolution, the coloration of the pronghorn is an excellent example of natural camouflage. The upper body is primarily a rich reddish-tan. The lower body, legs and a large patch on the rump are white. On a mature buck, the top of the nose up to the eyes and between the horns is commonly dark chocolate brown to black. On a doe, this area is most often dark brown to tan. Bucks can usually be distinguished by the black patch found on the upper throat and back of each jaw. Broken patches of white on the throat, brisket and often along the front of the shoulder complete nature's camouflage job.

Unless standing silhouetted on the horizon, pronghorns can often be extremely difficult to spot thanks to this patchwork of coloration. This is especially true on cloudy days when the white areas reflect less light. A light snow on the ground can make it even more difficult to detect pronghorns without the aid of binoculars. This is particularly true when the animals are bedded or standing in knee-high sagebrush.

HAIR. Compared to the hair found on deer and most other North American big-game species, the body hair of a pronghorn feels considerably stiffer and more coarse to the human touch. The pronghorn's body is covered with two layers of hair, made up of long guard hairs and a sparse underlayer of shorter hair. The guard hairs are cellular, meaning that they are air-filled. Again, evolution has created the perfect plains animal with the pronghorn. The hollow hairs allow the animal to withstand tremendous temperature extremes from winter to summer. When it's bitterly cold, these hairs lay close to the body, providing outstanding insulation. When summer temperatures soar upward, a unique system of muscles just under the hide allow the pronghorn to extend these hairs up and away from the skin, allowing cooling breezes to flow over the body surface. The layer of underhair is so fine that it is difficult to see. The hair found on the legs is also very short and sparse compared to the body hair.

Pronghorn molting

Pronghorns molt in the spring, appearing mangy-looking as the old pelage comes off to be replaced by new growth. During fall, the coloration of this handsome creature is at its brilliant best.

The hair of the distinct white rump patch is nearly twice as long as other body hair. These hairs, and the long guard hairs that make up the mane on the back of the neck, can be extended when a pronghorn is alarmed or excited. When the white rump hairs are fully erect, it creates what appears to be a white flash when viewed from a distance.

Although antelope seldom enter water, they can swim. Relatively sizeable rivers like the Missouri River may create a diversion for traveling antelope, but generally don't prevent pronghorns from moving into better winter or summer range. The hollow, cellular nature of the guard hair provides buoyancy.

Pronghorn hair is not firmly attached to the skin, and it can be easily pulled out or rubbed loose. More than one potential full shoulder mount has been ruined because the hunter dragged his trophy a short distance to the truck. Extra precaution should always be taken when handling antelope destined for a taxidermist's shop. Not only can contact with the ground during a short drag result in a hairless shoulder, rough handling can also break many of the brittle, hollow guard hairs.

HIDE. Due to the extremely large number of pronghorns roaming the plains at the time when market hunters were shooting the buffalo purely for their hides, considerable efforts were made to find a use for antelope leather. It was used on everything from hats and belts to shirts and saddle tack. In the end, it was determined that only an antelope had a real use for its own hide. Tanners and garment makers found the leather too porous and too weak to have any real commercial value.

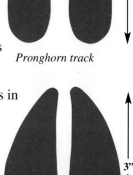
Pronghorn track

FEET AND LEGS. On relatively solid ground, the track of a pronghorn does not look all that much different than the track of a whitetail deer. A mature antelope buck track is about 2¾ inches in length, while the track of a whitetail buck is usually 3 to 3½ inches in length. The track of a pronghorn is noticeably narrower to the trained eye. In soft ground, the difference becomes obvious since the pronghorn doesn't have dew claws. The first and fourth digits of the feet are not developed; thus antelope have only two toes on each foot, and lack dew claws.

Whitetail track

To better absorb and cushion the shock of high running speeds, the pads of pronghorn hooves are thicker and more defined that those of a deer. The larger front hooves bear most of the weight, hitting the ground hardest when the animal is in full flight. Considering the pronghorn's running speed – known to top 60 mph – and the rough, rocky terrain that makes up much of the antelope's home range, one might expect to see quite a few of the animals with leg and hoof injuries. However, the seemingly delicate leg bones are surprisingly strong and resilient, enabling antelope to negotiate rough, uneven surfaces at all speeds with few injuries. Strength tests of pronghorn leg bones revealed that although they are about 10 times smaller than the leg bones of a domestic cow, they are nearly 40 times stronger. One test found that it took nearly 20 tons of pressures per square inch to crush a pronghorn leg bone. The legs are disproportionately long compared to the pronghorn's body size, which aids the attainment of high running speeds.

HORNS. The uniquely shaped head gear of the pronghorn separates this animal from all other horned, hooved animals of the world in two respects. First, the so-called horn is composed of keratinized or hardened hair formed over a softer bony core. While the material is the same as that of true horned animals, such as sheep and cattle, the pronghorn is the only horned animal that actually sheds its horns annually. All others continue to grow the same horn throughout their lives. Second, the American pronghorn grows the only horns that branch, forming the prong from which the animal gets its name.

The horns are black in color, and on a mature buck can measure around the curve anywhere from 10 to 15 inches in length, depending on the age of the pronghorn and where it lives. Exceptionally large horns may measure up to 18 inches in length, while a very few 20-inchers have been taken by hunters. The usual "trophy class" buck today is one in the 14- to 15-inch range.

The curvature and direction of the main beam of antelope horns varies in both shape and direction. The horns of a classic pronghorn buck commonly angle slightly forward at the base, curving inward and slightly rearward at the tips. The last ½ to ¾ inch of the tip can be somewhat translucent and void of black coloration on longer-horned bucks. These are often referred to as "ivory tips."

Buck after shedding one horn

Doe with horns

The short, flat and slightly concave prong protrudes from the main beam somewhere about halfway up the length of the horn. This normally thrusts forward and upward from the main beam. However, there have been plenty of pronghorn bucks taken with prongs which protrude rearward, and occasionally one is harvested with prongs going both forward and backward. Some female antelope also grow horns, but they are considerably smaller and much thinner. Seldom will the horns of a doe exceed 6 inches in length, and rarely do they prong.

An injury or collision that bends the soft bony core can result in radically abnormal horn growth. It is not uncommon for a freak-horned buck to have one or both horns growing out of the skull parallel to the ground or bending forward over one or both eyes. Such oddities are highly prized by some hunters.

Pronghorn buck with a deformed horn

Sometimes genetic traits for oddball horns are passed on to future generations.

So what accounts for the exceptional horn growth in some areas, but not in others? First of all, genetics are a major factor. Quality adult pronghorn tend to produce quality offspring. However, the quality of the forage found in an area throughout the year also plays an instrumental role.

Once the rut period is over, new horn growth begins on the bony core. This new growth starts at the upper end of the inner bony core, and as the new sheath continues to grow, it actually forces the older outer sheath to loosen and fall off. Throughout most pronghorn range, the old horns are shed by early December. Generally, the development of the new outer horn sheath takes about 4 months. However, some experts feel that the growth continues through most of the year, right up until the start of the rut, when a buck's hormones begin to kick into high gear.

If a harsh winter and deep snows hamper the pronghorn's ability to adequately graze and browse, especially during the first few months of new horn development, growth of the new outer sheath could be stunted. Winter in the northern latitudes can be a tough time for antelope, especially once snows begin to completely cover the ground with a 1- to 2-foot-deep blanket. If there is a forage problem during the winter, when most of a buck's reserves and nutrition must be used to survive, horn growth in that area suffers. Likewise, if a prolonged drought during the spring, summer and early fall affects the quality of the food supply, further horn development will be impeded.

Close-up showing the hardened hair of an antelope's horn

Greg Hyatt, a game manager for the Wyoming Game and Fish Department in the Rawlins area, has observed that following extreme summer drought conditions, antelope horns are short, skinny at the bases, and exhibit prongs that are lower on the main beam than normal. He acknowledges that certain areas continue to consistently produce high-quality bucks year after year. A few of these places predominate entries in the Boone and Crockett Club record book. In Hyatt's opinion, these areas are likely inhabited by pronghorns with exceptional genetics, but he also points out that these places must also excel in the quality, quantity and diversity of the forage.

SPEED. Which is faster, the cheetah or the pronghorn? No one really knows, because no one has ever witnessed a cheetah pursuing a pronghorn! Experts tend to agree that right out of the starting block, the cheetah enjoys a faster burst of speed. However, like most cats, the cheetah's high speed is short-lived and after just a few hundred yards this swift cat really begins to slow. The cheetah simply doesn't have the lung capacity for an extended run. On the other hand, the pronghorn has been built for speed. In fact, many wildlife experts consider it the fastest land runner on earth. A cheetah would be gasping for air and slowing before a pronghorn was fully wound out.

Speed is the pronghorn's number-one line of defense against predators. Pronghorns can cruise along effortlessly at 30 mph, and when excited or frightened may reach speeds in excess of 60 mph in an all-out burst. They can run nearly at full speed for up to 4 miles before becoming fatigued. And a leap at full speed can easily cover 25 or more feet.

Compared to other similar-sized animals, the pronghorn's heart and lungs are both oversized. Likewise, the windpipe is exceptionally large in diameter and allows a high volume of air intake with each breath. When running flat out, the pronghorn often appears to be gasping for air, running with its mouth open. In truth, the animal is simply using its mouth to increase the amount of air to the lungs. The nostrils alone are not large enough to allow an adequate flow of air for an animal which may be moving at 50 to 60 mph. Nature's special adaptations help promote the stamina needed for high-speed running.

One does not have to be around pronghorns long to realize that these creatures love to run, and will jump at the opportunity to race other moving objects such as vehicles, trains or even riders on horseback. They appear to be well aware of their considerable speed and readily enjoy showing it off. Many motorists have had a herd cruise alongside their car or pickup truck for a mile or more at 40 to 50 mph, only to have the antelope speed up and cross the road in front of them. No one really knows why they seem

to get such enjoyment out of outrunning vehicles. However, once they accomplish just that, it's not uncommon for them to stop abruptly and stare back arrogantly at their opponent, as if their point had been made. Then, it would not be unusual for the same herd to turn and run full speed right back to where the race had started.

Despite the pronghorn's ability to jump great lengths horizontally, rarely will they attempt jumping a fence that's just 3 feet high. Instead, a common trait is for pronghorns to run up to a barbed-wire fence, then crawl beneath the fence's bottom strand. An entire herd will often wait and crawl under such a fence one by one until all are on the other side. Where they cross under a fence on a regular basis antelope will wear a trench into the ground.

Woven-wire fences that go completely to the ground pose a real threat for pronghorns. Even though the animals are physically capable of leaping over the fence, entire herds have starved to death when trapped by deep snow in the corner of a woven wire fence simply because they could not crawl under it and they refused to jump it.

STOMACH. Pronghorns ingest a wide range of native grasses, agricultural crops and low brush. Its diet of high fiber and cellulose would not be digestible without a multiple-chambered stomach. Thus nature has provided this ruminant with a complex four-chambered stomach. Food is pre-processed in two of these chambers, then later regurgitated for final chewing and digestion in the other partitions of the stomach. As a cud chewer, the pronghorn eats and digests food in a similar way to deer and domestic cattle. In keeping with their general temperament, antelope can feed heavily for a short time, then chew their cud later during frequent rest periods. The animals have even been observed chewing their cud

BARBED-WIRE FENCES are usually not a problem for pronghorns as long as they can slip under the bottom strand. Unfortunately, a woven-wire fence (inset) totally blocks antelopes' movement because they can't crawl under it, and they almost always refuse to jump over it.

while sleeping. This efficient digestive system produces little waste relative to the volume of food consumed.

SENSES

SIGHT. The one thing a pronghorn hunter should always keep in mind is that if he can see the pronghorn, the pronghorn can certainly see him, unless the hunter is well concealed in a blind of sorts or has taken cover in thick sage or heavy, creek bottom foliage. It's practically a given that if you step out into the open and spot an antelope, you'll immediately discover that it's already looking in your direction. Many knowledgeable trophy hunters claim that the pronghorn's eyesight is equivalent to that of a human looking through 8-power binoculars. Although pronghorns are not particularly good at discerning

motionless objects or shapes, they can pick up the slightest movement from several miles away.

Their eyes, which measure nearly 2 inches in diameter, are located practically at the base of the horns. Due to the wide set of the eyes, which are literally on each side of the head, antelope enjoy nearly a 360-degree view of their surroundings. The animal's only blind spot is directly behind its head. When trying to slip within range of a quarry with such tremendous vision, the hunter usually finds the problem compounded by the fact that instead of just one set of these eyes, he's trying to make the move on a herd consisting of 10 to 40 animals, all blessed with the same keen eyesight.

SMELL AND HEARING. Antelope have a good sense of smell at intermediate ranges, but it is by no means as acute as that of the whitetail deer.

Prairie Race

Can antelope attain speeds of 60 mph? Yes they can!

An old hunting partner and I were once cruising a smooth two-track road that stretched across a fairly level stretch of eastern Wyoming. Out of a nearby arroyo poured a herd of about a dozen antelope. They appeared to be trying to cross the roadway immediately in front of us. Being the sport that he is, my buddy decided to give them a run for their money and stepped on the gas. The race was on!

At about 35 mph, the herd cruised along effortlessly next to us. My partner tapped his horn a couple of toots, and the little brown and white speedsters decided to really show their stuff and kicked it into passing gear. In no time, we were flying down that old two-tracker at 55, and those darn antelope were sticking with us. They laid their ears back and stretched those long legs for more territory. At nearly 60, we were still pacing each other. Then, there it was, a prairie speed bump in the form of a small unseen ditch.

The next thing I knew we were going airborne, then my head made contact with the roof of the pickup cab. Miraculously, the truck came back to earth, wheels down and still on the two-track course. Gear, including our two rifles, bounced all over inside the pickup, causing my friend to let up on the gas for just an instant. And that was all those pronghorns needed. In a flash the herd darted across the road right in front of us. Then, the antelope screeched to a halt and stood to stare at the two losers in the Ford pickup.

Do antelope enjoy racing moving vehicles? You bet they do!

– Don Oster

Experienced pronghorn hunters know that it's always advisable to approach from the downwind side during a stalk. While a pronghorn may go on alert when it picks up a human or foreign scent, it is so dependent on its eyesight that the animal will normally try confirming danger by sight before taking flight. Its hearing is also reasonably well developed. However, because of the wide open habitat they prefer, sight remains an antelope's prominent danger-detecting sense. They normally spot approaching danger long before picking up scent or detecting sounds. However, the bowhunter or muzzleloading hunter limited to close-range shooting must always keep scent and sound in mind when trying to slip close to a pronghorn.

A FINAL WORD

There is no way to put it delicately – pronghorns stink! The pungent, musky smell is one of the first things the beginning pronghorn hunter notices when admiring his first animal. Whether the smell is from glands on the body, the pronghorn's diet, perspiration from those hard high-speed runs or some other factor, these beautiful animals emit a highly offensive body odor. And this strong smell is likely why many hunters and western residents of the U.S.

commonly refer to them as "goats" or "prairie goats." The smell is found in both the horns and hide, and in excessive cases can be hard to mask on mounted heads. Thankfully, the smell does not permeate the meat, which is delicious providing it is given prompt, proper care. Part of this care includes cleanly dropping the animal with a single well-placed shot, field-dressing and skinning the animal as quickly as possible, then hanging the carcass in a cool place for several days. Do not allow the hair to make contact with the meat under any circumstance. For those long trips home, always quarter or bone the meat, and pack it in a container to keep it cool. When it's extremely hot, you may have to rely on using dry ice.

The eating quality of antelope and other wild game can get a bad rap due to improper care after the animal is harvested. Imagine harvesting a prime beef, field-dressing it, then loading it on top a vehicle. Drive with it out in the hot sun for several hundred miles, then tour it around town to show it off for a couple of days. After all that, take the carcass to the local locker plant to have it skinned and processed. How good do you think the choice cuts would taste?

History & Herd Restoration

What distinguishes the American pronghorn more than any other fact is that it is a single-species family, known as *Antilocapridae*. While it is often referred to as an antelope, the pronghorn is in no way related to the true antelopes of Africa. Fossil remains found in North America, some dating back nearly 20 million years, reveal that the pronghorn once existed as several distinct subspecies, some of which were as small as jackrabbits, while others were considerably larger than the pronghorn we know today. All subspecies shared two traits: they were dwellers of the open prairies, and they shed their horn sheaths annually. Today, some wildlife professionals recognize several subspecies (p. 8), while others claim these are simply the same animal with slight adaptations to a specific geographical area.

Long before the first human settlers of North America, the pronghorn ranged as far east as Illinois. However, by the time European settlers arrived on this continent, the pronghorn was found only west of the Mississippi River. Today, it occupies much of the same range, from the prairie provinces of southern Canada through the Plains and intermountain states of the U. S., and into the high plains of northern Mexico. Pronghorns are

well suited to the natural plains habitat of expansive open territory marked by buttes, large open draws and *arroyos* (water-carved gullies) covered by sage and a variety of native grasses.

The pronghorn is as much a part of our Western heritage as the buffalo. For nearly as long as the two have existed, they have roamed the plains together. Although estimates vary, as many as 50 to 60 million pronghorns may have roamed North America during precolonial times. If these estimates are accurate, it is possible that pronghorns may well have outnumbered the buffalo. Experts feel that the two enjoyed a symbiotic relationship before market and hide hunting decimated the great buffalo herds. Deep, heavy snows, which can cover the prairies and deprive today's pronghorn of much needed food sources, were less of a

problem when buffalo were still present in large numbers. The size and strength of the buffalo enabled them to plow through heavy snow drifts, keeping travel routes open for the much smaller pronghorn. And where the buffalo nosed its way down through deep snows to graze on the grasses beneath, the pronghorn would follow and find enough life-giving sustenance to survive even a brutal winter.

The American Plains Indian hunted the pronghorn, along with the buffalo, elk and mule deer, which also inhabited the plains. The technique known today as "flagging" was one of the Indian's favored antelope hunting tactics. These hunters discovered that the pronghorn's curiosity could be used to lure it in close enough to be taken with bow and arrow. They accomplished this by hanging or waving a piece of cloth or strip of light-colored buckskin just above the sagebrush or native grasses. The movement of the material would catch and hold the pronghorn's attention. And sooner or later, the animal would move in close to investigate the flicker of movement, presenting the patient hunter a close-range shot. Some modern-day hunters still rely on flagging to shorten the distance of their shot.

White man's first encounters with pronghorns probably took place when the first French "voyageurs" and fur trappers explored what later became the Louisiana Purchase. Members of the 3-year-long Lewis and Clark expedition, and the flow of white trappers known as "mountain men" that followed, relied heavily on the abundant supply of game found all along the Missouri River for food. In fact, designated hunters with Lewis and Clark were charged with keeping the larders full, providing up to 10 pounds of meat per man per day. While the majority of game harvested consisted of deer, elk and buffalo, these frontier hunters rarely turned down the opportunity to include a few pronghorns in their take.

Most of the members on the expedition sent out to explore America's newly acquired lands carried the .54-caliber Model 1803 U.S. flintlock rifle made at Harpers Ferry Armory, but a few brought along their own flintlock

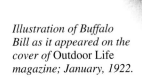

Illustration of Buffalo Bill as it appeared on the cover of Outdoor Life *magazine; January, 1922.*

Kentucky long rifles, which were usually of a smaller caliber. Effective range for any of these rifles and patched round ball projectiles was well under 100 yards, and they found that getting that close to the wary pronghorn was no easy task. Needless to say, the Lewis and Clark party didn't dine on antelope very often.

During precolonial times, pronghorn populations remained high, at levels that the range and available forage could support. The animals ranged freely, with natural land features like mountain ranges the only major physical barriers to impede their movement and range. The encroachment of settlers on the Plains and in the wide mountain valleys brought on massive land use changes and triggered the downfall of the West's vast herds of animals. The establishment of towns and cities, farms and ranches, and eventually roads and highways all resulted in the loss of critical habitat, especially wintering areas that traditionally provided for the animals during the cold, lean months. Woven-wire fences, railroad tracks, roadways and other human development mystified the animals and inhabited their freedom of movement. These changes equally impacted buffalo and pronghorn numbers. Simultaneously both were faced with habitat shrinkage and relentless, uncontrolled hunting pressure.

Often, wealthy eastern and European sportsmen travelled to the American West to shoot a few buffalo and pronghorns, but most of the early hunting in this region was subsistence hunting by settlers needing meat to feed themselves and a hungry family. Literally millions of buffalo and pronghorns were also slaughtered on the Plains by market hunters who shipped the meat back to the big metropolitan areas of the East, plus to growing settlements all along the great Rocky Mountains. At one time, three antelope carcasses had a market value of only 25¢. Laborers building the transcontinental railroads and miners also needed feeding, and the only way to provide fresh meat, especially in summer months, was continuous market hunting. One of the most famous market hunters was Buffalo Bill Cody, who with his crews of hunters, killed tens of thousands of buffalo and antelope for meat and hides. During a 1-month period, Cody relied on his favored .50-70 trapdoor rifle, which he nicknamed "Lucretia Borgia", to down more than 1,000 buffalo. Pronghorns, which benefited from the relationship with buffalo, were slaughtered right along with them. Other Plains species such as elk and mule deer adapted to the mountainous high country, escaping the invasion. Not so with pronghorns. They remained on the open prairie with the buffalo and were nearly hunted into extinction.

Railroads provided ready access to the western Plains, bringing settlers and others into antelope country. Shooting at pronghorns, buffalo and other game from moving rail cars became popular, and was considered great sport. General Phillip Sheridan led two highly publicized "sport" hunts on the Plains that were attended by rich industrialists, politicians, European royalty and other influential people, who shot numerous buffalo, antelope and elk. Many of these animals were simply left to rot. Sheridan and the U.S. Army encouraged the slaughter of game on the Plains as a means of conquering the Plains Indian tribes. They reasoned that if they could rid the Plains of the Indians' primary source of food, these indigenous people could easily be brought under control.

Much of what is considered "prime" pronghorn habitat offers minimal grazing for cattle. Large areas of Wyoming, for instance, can only graze 10 head of cattle per 1,000 acres. Due to the semi-arid nature of the region, the grass is extremely sparse, and traditionally has been for ages. Early pioneer-ranchers

Shooting antelope from a train in Colorado in the year 1875; illustration as it appeared in Outdoor Life *magazine, 1932.*

A Success Story

The success of pronghorn transplant and restoration programs can be seen in the following chart showing the census from the time re-introduction efforts began.

YEAR	PRONGHORN IN THE U.S.
1920s	30,000
1930s	130,000
1940s	250,000
1950s	360,000
1970s	400,000
1980s	400,000 to 500,000
1990s	500,000+

The biggest threat to continued growth of antelope populations in this country is the loss of habitat to human development. Fortunately, there remains a considerable amount of suitable habitat in a number of states, including Texas, Kansas, Nebraska, South Dakota and North Dakota, where the pronghorn once roamed, but into which this plains dweller has yet to be reintroduced. And as strange as it may sound, 40 pronghorns from Colorado have even been transplanted onto the Kissimmee Prairie of central Florida. Only time will tell.

believed that antelope represented serious competition with grazing livestock for the scarce pasture, and viewed them as pests. Many declared war on pronghorns, shooting them at will. Unfortunately, there are still a few ranchers who continue to feel that pronghorns consume too much of the protein-rich grasses also needed for raising cattle.

The demise of the pronghorn paralleled that of the buffalo, which had been reduced to less than 1,000 animals by the early 1890s. Between 1825 and 1900, antelope populations were reduced from somewhere between 40 and 60 million to between 10,000 and 30,000 animals. And these existed only in a few small scattered bands.

The number of pronghorns in North America remained stable, yet severely endangered, from the turn of the 20th century until the early 1920s. Although the dawning of a conservation conscience in the United States began as early as the late 1880s, the movement didn't gain substantial momentum until Theodore Roosevelt, an avid hunter and outdoorsman, became President in 1901. Then, a realization grew that game was not of an unending supply and that many species could be wiped out in the absence of responsible protection, care and management. It was the enactment of game regulations in the 1920s and 1930s that saved the pronghorn from extinction, by providing law-enforced protection for the few antelope that remained. These same laws also benefited countless other species of birds and animals, and were the beginning of modern wildlife management.

Unfortunately for the buffalo, roaming herds of animals that weigh 1,000 to 2,000 pounds at maturity were considered incompatible with man's use of the land. Except for the establishment of several herds in special set-aside areas, no attempts were made to re-establish the buffalo in a wild state. However, the much smaller 100- to 125-pound pronghorn, and its ability to more readily adapt to ranching and agricultural land use, presented the potential for restoration where suitable habitat could be found. It was the beginning of a new era, and through the mid-1900s responsible, professional and informed game management evolved. Much of it was based primarily on the studies and teachings of Aldo Leopold. It was a period of learning, and many of the earliest game managers thought that they need only provide protection for a species and it would thrive. Leopold pioneered game management principals based on the relationships between species and habitat, and the population-carrying capacity of habitat. These initial principles, coupled with protection, form the basis of game management practices today.

Early wildlife conservation and restoration efforts, including those for the pronghorn, were almost fully funded by private individuals and conservation-minded organizations. The Pittman-Robertson Act of 1937 marked the first and probably the only time when citizens (specifically sportsmen) insisted on paying taxes. These taxes were levied on the purchases of outdoor equipment, such as guns and ammunition. The funds raised were earmarked and allocated specifically to fund wildlife resource management efforts. The financial support provided is substantial and continues today. Return of the money to the states for specific projects has funded the reintroduction and reestablishment of many species of birds and game animals into most of their historic range. The successful rebuilding of pronghorn herds throughout the West is a prominent example of what can be accomplished when sound management programs receive the necessary funding.

Texas conservation officials successfully trapped and relocated antelope; photo as it appeared in Outdoor Life *magazine, 1940.*

The first successful live trapping and efforts to transplant pronghorns into suitable habitat were

Teenage Adventure

Other than the fact that I knew my two hunting partners and I were headed for Wyoming, my first pronghorn hunting trip did not entail a whole lot more planning. I was just 16 years old at the time, and my two companions were only a year older. We had grown up in west-central Illinois, and after reading a pickup load of old outdoor magazines, we had decided to try our hand at western big-game hunting. Antelope and mule deer seemed like logical choices, even though none of us had ever laid eyes on either species.

We had worked all summer for local farmers, and had earned the money for making the trip. Once our parents realized we were serious about the hunt, one of the other boys' fathers offered the use of his late-model pickup. We made arrangements with the school to be absent an entire week, and with all of our hunting and camping gear piled into the back of that truck, we struck out for Wyoming.

The year was 1965, and we were able to purchase our non-resident deer and pronghorn permits right over the counter at a Cheyenne sporting goods store for just $35 for each permit. The man who sold us our permits even told us of a rancher who might let us hunt. And once the landowner learned that three teenage boys had driven nearly a thousand miles to hunt deer and pronghorn, he simply couldn't refuse.

The next 6 days were an adventure I'll never forget. All three of us filled our deer tags with respectable 4x4 mulies, and we each tagged a good 14-inch class pronghorn. While we truly enjoyed the opportunity to hunt mule deer, it was the stalking, crawling, sneaking and long-range shooting required to take our antelope that we talked about all the way home. And when we did get back to our small, rural Illinois hometown, those pronghorns were the first any of the townspeople had ever seen.

I've been a pronghorn hunter ever since.

– Toby Bridges

started in the mid-1930s by T. Paul Russell in New Mexico. This pioneer of antelope restoration adapted the methods he used for catching antelope from the experience he had gained while live trapping wild horses. Some of these early methods included herding pronghorns into high fence corrals and entangling the animals in a wall of netting. Both proved effective, but tended to be rough on the frail, yet high-spirited antelope. Today's game managers rely on drop nets shot from helicopters to capture these fleet little animals for restocking.

Today, the number of pronghorns roaming the open spaces of the western U.S. has topped 500,000. The center of this population is found in Wyoming. Here we find the largest expanses of good pronghorn habitat, and a very sparse human population. Individual state game agencies closely monitor antelope population levels and herd density. In most states, hunting for pronghorns is micro-managed, meaning that the state, or the portion of the state where antelope are found, is broken up into smaller, well-defined hunting units. This allows the game departments to issue a given number of permits for a specific hunting unit, based on the number of antelope inhabiting a particular area. Huntable pronghorn populations exist in more than 15 states. In fact, the pronghorn can now be hunted in just about every state west of the Mississippi River, except for those states that actually border the river. In Wyoming, more than 100,000 permits are usually offered on an annual basis, while in a few states, such as California, pronghorn hunting is permitted on a very limited basis.

Modern management practices center around an annual harvest dictated by herd census within areas of each state and the carrying capacity of the available range. Harvests are controlled by a permit quota system within specified areas or management units of a state. Prospective hunters must apply for licenses within a given management unit, with successful applicants generally selected at random through a computer drawing. During the 1960s and early 1970s, antelope tags for both residents and non-residents could be purchased right over the counter in a few states. Those days are long past. As interest in hunting the pronghorn continues to increase, the odds of being drawn for one of the allotted permits for a particular area decrease. Many of the top big-buck-producing areas of New Mexico and Arizona offer only a small handful of permits each year, and getting drawn for one of these is nearly impossible.

The American Bison Society of Alberta, Canada, transplanted antelope to game preserves throughout the western U.S.; photo as it appeared in Outdoor Life *magazine, 1922.*

Growing Up

Pronghorns are unique, neat little animals. The more I have come to know them, the better I like them. I guess my love affair with pronghorns started somewhere at an early age, probably coming from reading magazine articles and looking at pictures of them.

Growing up as a youngster in southern Indiana, I didn't have any big-game hunting to enjoy. But I hunted small game with a passion, knowing that someday I would have the opportunity to go after bigger, more glamorous species. When other kids were starting to date, I was too busy fishing, frog hunting or chasing squirrels and rabbits. Following college, marriage and a job move to Texas, I started hunting whitetails, then made a few jaunts to Colorado for mule deer, and eventually jumped at the opportunity to hunt pronghorns in Wyoming, sometime in my late twenties.

I was hunting "antelope" the first time I ever saw a live one. And I collected the biggest one I've ever shot that very first day of hunting them.

My first hunt combined all the facets of hunting pronghorns, including a long-range spot, a long tedious stalk, lots of cactus in my hands and knees, and it ended with one well-placed shot. On this hunt, I learned what is probably the most important thing about hunting pronghorns – it is just one hell of a lot of fun!

– Don Oster

Habitat

"Home . . . home on the range. Where the deer and the antelope play."

This line from an old favorite western tune pretty well sums up the country where today you'll find the majority of pronghorns in North America. When we think of antelope, we picture a herd of animals racing at high speed across an open, endless prairie of grass and sage. While this is the most common habitat for pronghorns, they are also found in a few places where, at first sight, one would never expect to find this open-country dweller. For example, it's not unusual to occasionally find pronghorns inhabiting high country above 9,000 or 10,000 feet. And in some regions, they are found right down at sea level.

Pronghorn populations can be found ranging in every western state, in Alberta and Saskatchewan of Canada, and in northern Mexico. The eastern edge of the pronghorn range in the United States is a line running through the western Dakotas, Nebraska, Kansas, the panhandle of Oklahoma and western Texas. All states west of this line have a resident pronghorn population, with the largest numbers living in Wyoming, Montana and Colorado.

Several factors determine the quality of pronghorn habitat. One of the most important is the absence of barriers that could restrict free movement of the animals. In optimum habitat, which provides plenty of forage and which has an abundant water supply, the freedom to move great distances may not normally be necessary – not in a typical year anyway. However, during an unusually harsh winter or a prolonged drought, pronghorns may need to relocate to find suitable food or water sources. While antelope do not migrate in the true sense of the term, they will move 50 or more miles if necessary to find food and water.

The most common barrier found on pronghorn range has to be the fence. As a rule, barbed-wire fences do not pose a big threat to pronghorn movement. As long as the bottom strand is well above ground level, the antelope will merely slip beneath the lower strand. But barbed wire stretched just 8 to 10 inches above the ground can seriously impede pronghorn movement.

The Bureau of Land Management, which administers much of the pronghorn's prime habitat, requires that the bottom strand of barbed wire on any of its lands be a minimum of 16 inches (in most cases) above the ground. This provides an ample gap for pronghorns to crawl through. Where several different herds cross beneath a fence once or twice a day for a year or more, they actually wear out a trench that gives them more room for getting from one side to the other. Woven-wire fences, or "sheep fences" as they are often referred to, can and will stop antelope movement unless the animals can find a hole to crawl through.

Other barriers that can become obstacles to antelope movement include interstate highways, towns, subdivisions, shopping centers and other major human developments. Any of these barriers can block access to suitable forage and water in hard times, and seriously threaten a herd's ability to adapt and survive through the tough periods.

Another factor that determines the quality of pronghorn habitat is the diversity of the forage found there, primarily the quality and quantity of broadleaf plants. While antelope can be classified as opportunity feeders, which will consume around a hundred different plants and shrubs, their preferred forage is mostly made up of protein-rich native prairie forbs along with sagebrush, bitterbrush, saltbush, and even western juniper. Irrigated or river bottom agricultural crops, including winter wheat, clover and alfalfa, add to the diversity of the food supply and will be heavily grazed by pronghorns when needed. Protein-rich

sage is common to most ideal antelope habitat, and provides valuable winter browse. Contrary to popular belief (or unpopular belief among cattle and sheep ranchers) the pronghorn's diet actually consists of very little grass. The native grasses that are grazed by livestock make up only a small part of an antelope's annual diet. The vast majority of suitable pronghorn habitat consists of rolling wide plains found at 3,000 to 6,000 feet above sea level. And because their primary protection from predators includes the ability to see long distances, the best habitat is usually very open. However, this is not to say that pronghorns will not be encountered in the broken and partially forested areas commonly found at 7,000 to 9,000 feet throughout much of their range. In many areas, herds establish both a summer and winter range, which may be only a few miles apart, but also separated by several thousand feet in elevation. When pronghorns do inhabit higher, often forested habitat, they are most likely to be found frequenting the open, grassy parks and meadows.

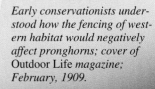

Early conservationists understood how the fencing of western habitat would negatively affect pronghorns; cover of Outdoor Life *magazine; February, 1909.*

High-Altitude Antelope

One of the problems with having to travel halfway across the country to hunt pronghorns is that it doesn't give one much time to spend scouting. So during an early October combination mule deer and antelope hunt, my hunting partner and I made the most of the day prior to the season opener and spent every hour of daylight glassing the sage-covered flats stretching out from the base of Wyoming's Snowy Range. Before the sun set that evening, we had easily looked at 400 to 500 antelope, including several bucks with horns that would top 15 inches.

Our plans were to first spend 3 or 4 days hunting mule deer on a high broken plateau nearly 2,000 feet higher, but less than 10 miles away. Then we would return to the lower sage flats to hunt pronghorns.

In the first light of the next morning, I slowly made my way up the side of a sparsely forested ridge, stopping every half-mile to glass the open meadows and hay fields below. I was amazed at how many antelope were up "on top", at more than 8,000 feet elevation. An hour later, I spotted a good 15-inch-plus buck and thanks to the very broken terrain, I made an effortless stalk to within 150 yards and easily filled my tag with my super-accurate Sako .270 Winchester. Then, just 30 minutes after field-dressing the pronghorn, I pulled the trigger on a good mulie buck. My season was over.

When I returned at noon to where I had planned to meet my partner, I found him there waiting with a similar tale. He too had taken a good 15-inch pronghorn and managed to fill his deer tag as well. We spent a couple of days taking care of the meat and getting in some trout fishing. Then we headed home without ever firing a shot in what is considered classic pronghorn habitat.

– Toby Bridges

To support antelope herds, water must be available every 1 to 5 miles. Studies in Wyoming show that pronghorn herds were normally found to range no farther than 3 to 4 miles from a reliable water source. Depending on the time of the year, antelope need water in varying quantities. During the spring and early summer, when most of their food sources are lush and succulent, pronghorns can derive much of their daily moisture needs directly from the plants they feed upon, requiring only an additional 1 or 2 quarts of water. Summer and early fall can be dry, with hot drying winds and forage that has lost most, if not all, of its moisture content. Winter can also create greater demands for water. During these periods, the pronghorn's daily water need may be as high as 1½ gallons per day, which they get by eating snow.

Across most of the pronghorn's northern range, snowfall is a common annual occurrence. As a rule snow does not become a serious threat to antelope survival until it begins to accumulate deeper than 10 to 12 inches. Even when temperatures plummet to below zero for extended periods of time, pronghorns can withstand the cold – as long as they have access to adequate forage. Fresh snow a foot or more deep that can be easily pawed through to reach the grass and browse below doesn't tend to hamper the pronghorn's feeding ability. However, snow that crusts due to minor thaws and hard refreezes can create real problems.

Relative to their size, pronghorns have strong legs, which allow them to reach those ground-smoking

The third factor that is vital to pronghorn habitat is a reliable source of water. As a rule, all antelope habitat is arid to semi-arid with an average annual rainfall of just 10 to 15 inches. The largest expanses of the best pronghorn habitat in the U.S. are found in the area that comprises most of Wyoming, portions of Colorado and southern Montana. The region is broken by mountain ranges and heavy forests at the higher elevations. However, the majority of this region is made up of seemingly endless high plains, with sedge-covered draws and mesas. The combination of rolling prairies, great expanses of sagebrush and abundant, accessible water sources make this country ideal pronghorn habitat.

top speeds when running at full tilt. However, their small size and light weight work against them when faced with trying to paw through a layer of crusted snow and ice to reach feed below. When they do finally get through the crust on a foot or more of snow, they get easily bogged down, making them easy prey for predators such as coyotes and bobcats which can run across the hard, crusted surface.

Even when the snow doesn't crust over, extremely deep snow can completely cover food. It also makes it difficult or impossible for an animal the size of a pronghorn to travel any distance to find food and water. Weakened by hunger and thirst, struggling through deep snow drifts, and feeling the effects of bitter cold on a malnourished animal, the pronghorn becomes vulnerable to predators. Under normal winter conditions, predators usually prey on only the sick and injured. Every 8 to 10 years, deeper-than-normal snow that covers the ground for unusually long periods, or snow that becomes heavily crusted, can result in severe winter-kill in some northern areas. In fact, the primary factor that has caused the Wyoming pronghorn population to yo-yo up and down so dramatically has been winter-kill.

Pronghorns living at higher elevations in states like Idaho and Oregon must make an annual migration to low country as soon as snow levels reach a critical point, covering food supplies. Severe blizzards with accompanying high winds, drifting snow and bitterly cold temperatures have driven herds of antelope into towns as they search for water and food. These conditions and a resulting winter-kill can do serious damage to the population of a specific area with the effects lasting for several years.

Thanks to the outstanding insulating qualities of the pronghorn's long, air-filled guard hair, which covers the majority of its body, this well-adapted creature can withstand extremely low winter temperatures. But only if it enters the winter months in good condition. A poor forage base, resulting in a herd with low energy reserves under sub-standard conditions as winter approaches, makes the animals vulnerable to a winter die-off.

Not all pronghorns enjoy the ideal range found mostly in and around the state of Wyoming. But while they may not be thriving in some marginal habitat, the pronghorn continues to live in less-than-ideal locations. For example, in much of New Mexico the herds have adapted to extremely sparse vegetation, sometimes feeding on cedar or cactus when preferred foods are in short supply. The animals in the far Southwest ranging down into Sonora seldom need to cope with snow, but prolonged droughts do represent a real threat to antelope survival. Fortunately, cattle ranching in some of these areas now provides adequate water, thanks to deep wells and stock tanks. Still, the quality of the forage remains a problem in desert or near-desert habitat. The pronghorn's ability to live in habitat and terrain ranging from high mountains and foothills to desert areas speaks well for the adaptability of this incredible game animal.

Pronghorn doe and fawn

Food & Water Requirements

Nature has a way of keeping wild things in balance, and pronghorn population densities in any given area can be directly related to the availability of quality forage and easy access to a reliable, continuous source of water. Antelope nutritional needs are best met by a wide variety of broadleaf plants, and if suitable habitat is bordered by or intermingled with agricultural areas, so much the better. The diversity of food sources is often the key to a healthy resident herd of antelope.

The animals must have sources for highly nutritional forage on a year-round basis. In late winter and early spring, does must have access to quality forage preceding fawning to insure the health of their newborns. Areas that boast the highest fawn survival rates consistently provide the best quality food sources. It also stands to reason that healthy, well-fed animals that go into winter with high energy reserves will cope with harsh weather much better than pronghorns that have been forced to feed on less-than-adequate forage.

the most urgent need to feed heavily during late fall to recharge their systems before the onset of winter. Deep, early snows, which severely hamper the pronghorns' ability to feed, can prove to be extremely detrimental to pronghorn buck survival. These conditions likely explain why the mature-buck-to-mature-doe ratio in some areas can be as lopsided as 1:15 or 1:20.

FOOD TYPES. Pronghorns have been observed eating just about everything that grows on the western plains and prairies. They eat virtually anything that grows, which may be one of the reasons why so many people seem to enjoy calling them "goats" or "prairie goats." Truth is, antelope thrive where there is a diverse menu of healthy broadleaf plants and forbs to carry them through most of the seasons, especially where there is also a variety of browse to be consumed through the fall and winter months.

Buck feeding on sagebrush

Sage, or more correctly, sagebrush (*Artemisia tridentata*) and antelope go together. In fact, "sagebrush flats" and "pronghorn habitat" are essentially synonymous. Sagebrush can be found throughout almost all of the antelope's range and makes up an important part of the animal's diet. This hardy undershrub seems to do well in highly alkaline soil, and can be found covering vast tracts of the High Plains of the western U.S. It is a staple food source for pronghorns during winter when many other foods are not available or have been covered by deep snow. The woody plant provides an important source of protein, fat and carbohydrates. Sagebrush, along with other browse such as juniper, saltbush and rabbitbush, makes up nearly 80 percent of the pronghorn's winter diet where these plants are plentiful in an area. When such winter browse is absent, pronghorns often turn to agricultural crops such as winter wheat.

Run down and weakened from the rut, bucks must try to rebuild their energy reserves by feeding on highly nutritional forbs and shrubs. Where late fall and early winter forage is of low quality, many bucks will have difficulty reaching full horn potential the following year. Quality horn growth is directly related to quality forage, especially through the fall and winter.

A herd entering the winter season where there has been sufficient forage through the fall months generally enjoys a high over-winter survival rate. Because of their weakened condition as the rut draws to an end, mature bucks are most susceptible to winter die-off. While all antelope tend to go on a feeding spree when fall temperatures begin to drop, dominant males have

Favored antelope forage includes clover, dandelions, wild peas, chicory, larkspur, lupine and many other species of weeds or forbs that are consumed in quantity during the spring and summer. Pronghorns are definitely opportunity feeders. During the course of just about any day, they are likely to feed on any of more than a hundred known types of plants and grasses.

Where pronghorn population densities are the highest (particularly in Wyoming) the animals are extremely visible, and spend a great deal of time feeding. Most of the antelope observed from a passing vehicle seem to have their heads perpetually down, feeding like a herd of living lawn mowers. Since the earliest ranching ventures of the 1800s, cattle and sheep ranchers have waged war on pronghorns, claiming that the animals consumed tremendous quantities of grass that was needed by their livestock. The fact is, however, that grasses lack the high protein content needed by antelope and consequently are the least-consumed food on their menu. Studies have revealed that grass constitutes less than 10 percent of their annual diet. When pronghorns do feed on grass, it's mostly in the spring when the lush new growth contains a good amount of water.

FEEDING HABITS. Pronghorns feed frequently both day and night, and tend to feed for longer periods than deer. In fact, researchers have found that an antelope's stomach is nearly always full.

Pronghorns are constantly, nervously running here and there, playing or traveling to a water source. As they move about, they graze and browse almost continuously, taking nips of food from the most tender shoots of plants. Pronghorns do not have upper teeth but still make clean bites by pinching grasses or branch tips of favorite browse between their lower teeth and hardened, toothless upper gum.

Their feeding activity is regularly broken by short rest periods, during which they usually lay down and chew their cud. In the heat of a hot summer day, antelope seek an area with shade or with cooling breezes and spend much of the day lazily laying about. At this time of the year, they do most of their feeding during early morning, late evening and during the night. While pronghorns may spend much of a summer night feeding, they don't tend to move as far in the dark as whitetail deer. They are not habitual nocturnal roamers or feeders. If there is a bright full or nearly full moon, antelope will move more at night than during the dark of a new moon.

WATER. In order for any area to sustain a pronghorn population, water is a necessity. The pronghorn is now thriving in many places where population densities were once very sparse. A great example can be found in Sublette County, Wyoming. Much of this area is made up of rough, rolling, sagebrush-covered plains that are administered by the Bureau of Land Management. The Green River flows practically through the center of this county, and has, through the ages, provided for pronghorn and other wildlife species. However, once you get 5 or 6 miles away from the river, about the only sources of water are windmill-driven wells. These wells pump the life-giving liquid to the surface, where it collects in large metal stock tanks and small ponds, which are often created by the overflow.

Windmill wells can now be found every 3 or 4 miles, providing plenty of water for the cattle that graze there, as well as the pronghorn. While pronghorns are known to have inhabited the area long before the establishment of these wells, their need for water in the otherwise waterless region meant that they did not live there year-round. Today, there are numerous resident herds living the entire year here, always within a few miles of a well.

Studies in several areas by the Wyoming Game and Fish Department found that around 95 percent of more than 12,000 antelope monitored established a home range that offered a constant supply of water inside of a 3- to 4-mile radius. Much of this water comes in the form of wells for providing water to grazing livestock. Ranching has been good for pronghorns, but this too has had its price. While water became available through man's efforts, to once pronghorn-uninhabited arid areas, fences came along with the package – often limiting the free-roaming antelope's access to parts of good habitat. Fortunately, during the mid-1960s, regulations governing grazing rights on public lands established that ranchers could not erect "antelope-proof" fences on federal land. In a state like Wyoming, where close to 50 percent of the pronghorn habitat is found on public-owned land, this regulation has had a definite, positive impact on pronghorn numbers and distribution.

During the spring months, antelope can meet some of their daily moisture needs from the green, succulent vegetation consumed. This is usually supplemented with an additional quart or so of drinking water. However, since the antelope's habitat is primarily arid to semi-arid in nature, most of the year the animals become extremely reliant on a steady water source, and they will consume up to 1½ gallons of water each day. The highest water consumptions are during the heat of late summer, through a dry fall and into winter.

In most decent pronghorn habitat, they'll go to water at least once a day, and where they are not disturbed,

Pronghorns finding water at a windmill well

many herds will water twice a day. It's easy to see why a ground blind set near a water hole, or along a main access trail leading to a water hole, can be a surefire hunting tactic. In some areas it's the only way to get within bow or muzzleloader range of such a sharp-eyed quarry.

COMPETITION FOR FOOD. During precolonial times, the buffalo and the pronghorn made a nice, noncompetitive team of grazers. While the buffalo dined mainly on the native prairie grasses, the pronghorns routinely ate all the other stuff. As ironic as it may seem, once the buffalo had been virtually

eradicated from the plains, pronghorns did not greatly benefit from the flourishing prairie grasses. In fact, without the millions of buffalo to keep the grasses closely cropped, in many areas the grass grew higher than a man's head. The lush growth would not only impede the pronghorn's ability to spot approaching danger, but left unchecked, the abundant grasses actually crowded out much of the pronghorn's normal food supply.

When antelope feed on plants they take clean bites, actually snipping off shoots or buds. Their method of feeding does not damage the plants, and this natural pruning encourages fast, new growth. Even large herds have little discernible effect on the quality of food on range shared with domestic grazing animals.

The pronghorns' habit of feeding on the go, taking nips here and there as they move through a variety of

forage, makes it almost impossible to overgraze a reasonably sized parcel of land. On the other hand, cattle tend to destroy the plants they feed upon. These aggressive grazers bite and pull at grasses when feeding, very often uprooting the plants or severely damaging the plants' root structure. Even where cattle have severely overgrazed pastures, antelope can subsist on range that is too sparse for domestic livestock. When cattle have been removed from overgrazed land, leaving the pronghorn as the only inhabitant, it has been found that native grasses generally make a dramatic comeback.

Since across the West most of the prime antelope habitat is privately owned, multiple-use range land, we can only hope that ranchers will at least continue to tolerate the pronghorn's presence and consider them, at worst, minor pests that do very little damage to the range.

In light of the fact that pronghorns are actually good for the propagation of native prairie grasses, wise range managers should encourage antelope populations to live on their lands. Just as native grasses that were left unchecked once crowded out the pronghorn's favored forage plants, the same can happen if forbs and shrubs are left unchecked to take over open areas where grasses thrive. Because of their strong preference for plants which are generally undesirable forage for domestic livestock, antelope can help keep many of the unwanted plants in check. In addition, pronghorns readily eat many plants that are poisonous to domestic livestock but not to themselves. These plants include loco weed, larkspur, rubber weed, rayless goldenrod, cockleburs needle, thread grass, yucca, snakeweed, Russian thistle and saltbush.

ECONOMIC BENEFITS. Although they once complained about the ever present herds of smelly "prairie goats" on their cattle range, ranchers in northeastern Wyoming recently were at the forefront in urging the Game and Fish Department to tighten management controls and further limit hunter harvest. It seems that these landowners have finally realized that the once poorly regarded pronghorns do offer significant economic benefits through hunters' dollars. Almost as soon as they perceived the decrease in herd size in that portion of the state, due to several harsh winters and the resulting heavy winter-kill, they began demanding steps be taken to rebuild the pronghorn herd.

ACCESS FEES for self-guided hunts and fully guided antelope hunts are a great source of additional income for many ranchers in the West.

Throughout North America, big-game hunting has become big business. And with the current interest in pronghorn hunting, and the limited opportunities to hunt this animal (in comparison to deer), ranchers have discovered a new source of annual income. Thirty years ago, you could stop just about at any ranch and obtain permission to hunt antelope for free. Today, that same land has a price tag, either through an access fee for a self-guided hunt, or a sizeable sum for a fully guided hunt. In some of the better big-buck areas of the Southwest, a true trophy hunt can cost several thousand dollars.

Wyoming Water Hole

As I approached the small cluster of tents and campers sitting literally out in the middle of nowhere, surrounded by several hundred thousand acres of sagebrush-covered Bureau of Land Management range, I had to chuckle. Never before had I looked upon a more mismatched bunch of camping equipment in my life. In all, nearly two dozen of us had driven from seven different states to share this middle-of-nowhere camp during the muzzleloader season in Wyoming's antelope management unit 90. That night someone placed a small sign on a pole along the dusty two-track that passed within 50 feet of the camp: it read "Welcome to Musketville, Pop. 23."

The next day, we broke up into small groups of two and three and headed out in every direction to thoroughly scout our vast public hunting area. We all saw good bucks, but the area where we spotted the greatest concentration of antelope was a wide, nearly flat valley that ran up to a windmill-operated well barely a half-mile from camp. Every time we returned to camp, or sat in camp for an hour or longer, a herd of antelope would come to the shallow pond at the base of the stock tank to drink. Before dark, we chopped enough sagebrush to make a comfortable blind just 30 yards from the thirst-quenching water.

Our first hunter in the blind the next morning was there just an hour before dropping his 14-inch buck with a .54-caliber flintlock long rifle. The second hunter to use the blind stepped in at a few minutes before noon, then walked out to admire his buck about 2 hours later. The third hunter in the blind that day sat the rest of the afternoon and passed on three different 13-inchers, then returned the next morning to get an easy shot at a beautiful 14½-inch pronghorn. About midday the next morning, a fourth buck was taken from that blind, and 2 days later the best buck of the 23 harvested during our hunt was shot out of the same blind. In 5 days of muzzleloader hunting, five good bucks were taken from the same water hole, and the longest shot made was barely 50 yards.

Those hunters who had filled their tags would sit in the shade of a canopy back at camp and watch the show through binoculars. One commented, "It's almost as fun as shooting a good buck yourself!"

- Toby Bridges

Growth & Development

Unlike whitetails, pronghorns within a specific geographical area commonly share the same maturity timing. Why? While the factors are many, the primary reason is the length of a doe's estrus cycle and resulting condensed birthing period of pronghorn fawns.

FAWN DEVELOPMENT. A pronghorn doe has a single, and very short, estrus period in the fall. As a result, almost all fawns in any given area are born in a 2- to 3-week period in the spring. It is possible to travel through pronghorn country in the spring and see every doe without a fawn, then travel through the same area 2 weeks later and witness nearly every doe with one or two fawns. The short birthing period, just like every other facet of pronghorn life, is dictated by the very structured biology of this fascinating animal.

The rut in the northernmost reaches of the pronghorn's range often begins in late August; in the southernmost reaches, about early November. In the state of Wyoming, which is nearly in the center of this range, most fawns are born between late May and early June, following the normal 258-day gestation period.

While it is not uncommon for fawn of the year whitetail does to enter estrus, thus creating or contributing to a second or third rut period, pronghorn does do not reach sexual maturity until their second fall. Also, since whitetail does biologically can be bred over a 4 or 5 month period, the birthing period can cover the same time span, with fawns being born from April through July in some areas. This explains why it is not unusual to see a whitetail with spots even when the fall gun seasons open.

Pronghorns and whitetails do share one reproductive trait, and that's the fact that does giving birth for the first time generally have a single fawn. After that, twins are most common. And among pronghorns and whitetails, a healthy mature doe can give birth to triplets, although it's unusual. Antelope does that are not

bred during the short rut period, or are bred but fail to conceive, go without any offspring that next year.

At birth, a pronghorn fawn commonly weighs 4 to 6 pounds. Like almost all newborns, an antelope fawn is extremely vulnerable to predators such as the coyote and even eagles. Instinctively, the mother doe selects a secluded location for giving birth, concealing the fawn in cover, which is commonly close to higher ground where the doe can watch for approaching danger.

If the doe has twins, she will probably have them in separate locations that can be watched over from the same bit of high ground. By separating the two fawns she reduces the chances of both youngsters being killed by any predator that would happen upon them. Almost as soon as she gives birth, the doe retreats to the nearby vantage point where she can keep watch over the location of her young. Within an hour of birth, the fawns are able to stand on shaky legs and nurse. And as soon as the doe is confident that there is no impending danger, she slips down

quietly from her lookout to nurse the fawn or fawns. She continues doing this at intervals during the day, then returns to her vigil. If a predator or other threat approaches the location, she defends her young vigorously, striking out at predators with her sharp front hooves.

Nature has blessed the adult pronghorn with a natural camouflaged coloration that can make it difficult to spot these animals at any distance whatsoever. The light gray coloration of a newborn antelope

Yearling buck

fawn makes it still harder to see, even from up close. Unless the fawn moves, it blends right in with the ground, grasses, sagebrush, or any other foliage native to the area. More times than not, a fawn lets a man on foot or even a coyote pass within a few feet and never gives away its presence. Pronghorn fawns' bodies do not give off a scent for the first few days after birth, making it hard for predators to smell them.

Newborn fawns generally remain at or within close proximity of their birthing location for around 3 weeks. Within 2 days of birth, fawns can walk reasonably well, and by the third day can normally make short, awkward runs. By the end of their first week, pronghorn fawns begin to run and play, displaying early signs of the speed and agility they will later enjoy as adults. Occasionally the fawns may follow the doe for short periods during the second week, but since they would be unable to keep up with her if she were forced to flee at a full run, they're kept close to protective cover. The youngsters learn early in life to hide and remain motionless at the first sign of danger. Later in life, these same animals will rely on their keen eyesight and high-speed running abilities to keep plenty of distance between them and potential threats.

During their third and fourth weeks of life, fawns begin to follow the doe for longer periods, often rejoining the herd with her. At 6 weeks they begin to graze and browse, but continue to nurse. It is not until they are 4 months old that they are fully weaned, ending their dependence on the mother doe. From this point on, the fawns are fully capable of living on their own, but usually continue to follow the doe throughout their first year. By the time they are 3 months old, pronghorn fawns begin to display some of the adults' body coloration. At 1 year of age, yearling does can be distinguished from adult does by their slightly smaller body size. At the same time, yearling bucks begin growing their horns.

HORN GROWTH. All across the pronghorn's range, yearling bucks typically grow horns that are approximately the height of their 4- to 5-inch ears. Throughout the rest of their lives, the size of the head gear they adorn is influenced by many factors, not the least of which is the quality and quantity of the forage found within their habitat.

Many of the largest Boone and Crockett record book bucks harvested have come from areas of the Southwest, specifically from the states of Arizona and New Mexico. A number of 17-, 18-, 19-, and even a few 20-inch horned bucks have come from these states. While it may seem that these antelope are the products of superior genetics, the phenomenal horn growth is still related to both the quality and

Two-year-old buck with horns measuring 8 to 9 inches

quantity of the forage. Keep in mind that seldom does the weather in the arid to semi-arid regions of the Southwest become nearly as harsh or last as long as winter weather conditions found across Wyoming, Montana and into the southern plains of Alberta and Saskatchewan. Antelope inhabiting the southern regions of their range generally have considerably easier access to food supplies during winter than do their northern cousins, who may be faced with deep snows and crusted ice conditions. Winter can take its toll on pronghorns, and when winter forage is difficult to reach and in short supply, just surviving the bitter cold can demand every mouthful of forage eaten, leaving little nutrition for accelerated horn growth.

Southern pronghorns suffer their share of hardships as well. Prolonged droughts, which can hit the Southwest in May and June, often have a negative impact on fawn survival through the summer months. The lack of adequate rainfall normally means that forage condition also suffers, and during severe drought conditions water sources may begin to dry. Poor habitat conditions due to drought through spring, summer and fall may result in antelope entering the winter in less-than-perfect condition. This also affects horn development, especially the following year. Poor forage and overall range conditions typically result in horn growth that is thin at the base, short in beam length, and with prongs that are noticeably smaller and which grow closer to the base.

While researchers and biologists have never established a norm for "age vs. horn size," it is generally accepted that a 2-year-old pronghorn buck will likely have horns of about 8 inches in length. At 3 years of age most bucks have 12- to 13-inch horns, or slightly more where optimum forage exists. Antelope bucks that are 4 to 5 years old are considered to be in their prime, usually having the longest horn growth of their life. Horns measuring 15 inches in length from the outside base around the curl to the tip are considered a very good trophy. In fact, hundreds of 15-inch-class bucks can be found in the Boone and Crockett Club record book, including one buck taken in Weld County, Colorado, in 1965, which held the No. 4 spot in that book for years. That 15-inch-class buck scored 91⅜ B&C points.

Given the opportunity to reach 4 and 5 years of age, just about any pronghorn buck occupying good habitat with high-quality forage has the potential to reach true trophy stature. Pronghorn bucks that live beyond age 5 generally do not exhibit further horn growth. In fact, studies have proven that throughout most pronghorn habitat, bucks living beyond 5 years generally begin to experience less horn growth. Withered, unusually shaped horns are not uncommon on bucks

Three-year-old buck with 13- to 14-inch horns

Mature 4- or 5-year-old buck with horns measuring about 16 inches

WINTER-KILLED PRONGHORNS are often found once the snow melts in the spring.

which enter "old age" at 8 or 9 years old. Modern herd management programs and hunting regulations, which are aimed at keeping herd size within the carrying capacity of the range, ensure that most bucks are harvested or die by other means before reaching the end of their fifth year.

MORTALITY. The mortality rate for antelope fawns is the highest during the first 2 months, and in some regions can top 50 percent. Predators represent the leading cause of death. Coyotes, which are plentiful in pronghorn habitat, easily dine on more newborn pronghorns than all other predators combined. Often running in pairs or small packs, coyotes will work draws and valleys in spring to flush fawns out of hiding. When two or more coyotes take chase after a fawn that's less than a month old, it becomes easy prey. Other predators that also feed upon antelope fawns are bobcats, mountain lions, black bears and even an occasional eagle.

Once a pronghorn reaches 3 to 4 months of age and can run right along with the adults, predation becomes less of a threat as long as the herd is in a good, healthy condition. Predators always eliminate the sick and injured. When deep or crusted snows limit the pronghorns' mobility, predators can take an occasional adult antelope.

Deep snow is probaby the leading cause of adult antelope mortality. This is especially true when weather conditions warm enough to melt the surface of a foot or more accumulation, then dropping temperatures refreeze the surface to form a rock-hard crust. Once snows reach 12 to 15 inches in depth, pronghorns already have difficulty pawing through the deep blanket to reach forbs and grasses below. Faced with an extremely hard crust, the animals run into greater hardship breaking through a surface that often will support their weight. And when they do break through, pronghorns can become bogged down, making them easy prey for predators. In extremely deep, crusted snow, a pronghorn may not be able to climb back onto the surface, and could be trapped there until it starves. Deep snows that cover food supplies and limit movement to other suitable locations contribute directly to starvation. Many antelope have perished within sight of food and water they could not reach.

Manmade obstacles such as fences and highways also cause some accidental pronghorn deaths. Other minor causes of antelope mortality include drowning and miring down in muddy areas. However, year in and year out, winter continues to be the number-one cause of pronghorn mortality. Wyoming game manager Greg Hyatt says, "Once he reaches adulthood, a pronghorn buck will either be gotten by winter or a bullet!"

Among pronghorn managers, the general consensus is that a limited amount of winter-kill is generally good for the overall long-term health of an antelope herd. Normal winter conditions, especially in the northern climes, effectively weed out the weaker animals, leaving only the strongest to carry on the next year's breeding. A series of mild winters with no or little loss to the weather contributes to the survival of too many inferior animals within a herd. Overpopulation can lead to overuse and deterioration of the habitat, resulting in a generally weakened herd. Following an extended period of mild winters, a number of years, and several harsh winters, may pass before a herd recovers to a balanced, healthy state.

Throughout most northern antelope habitat, spring and summer forage is more than adequate, ensuring plenty of nutrition for fawn survival. Population lows are not normally a problem, and without some amount of winter-kill on an annual basis, the number of pronghorns would soon surpass the carrying capacity of the land. In the southern portion of antelope range, spring and summer drought conditions generally determine how many new pronghorns join the population.

An extended drought adversely affects the quality and quantity of forage, therefore it also affects the overall condition of the animals as well. The prenatal nutrition of does within a herd bears heavily on the health and survival of the year's fawn crop. Weakened, malnourished does will often abort rather than attempt birth. A pronghorn doe that is in very poor condition sometimes refuses to nurse her fawns, conserving the energy for her own survival.

Antelope are not widely affected by common bovid diseases. Parasites such as lice and ticks can leave

A DEPENDABLE WATER SOURCE is vital for the overall physical health of bucks, does and fawns.

some animals in an extremely weakened condition, often leading to diseases such as pneumonia, which makes survival in the antelopes' world difficult.

In healthy condition in good habitat, the average life expectancy for a pronghorn is 4 to 6 years. An animal that's 8 is very old, though one pronghorn has been documented to have lived to the ripe old age of 12.

Wyoming Winter

The winter of 1983-84 had been a tough one for Wyoming wildlife. Deep, never-ending snows had taken a tremendous toll on both pronghorns and mule deer, and after receiving word that the area around Rawlins had suffered a 50 percent winter-kill of pronghorn, I was surprised to learn that the scheduled antelope season in those management units would still take place.

I had drawn a pronghorn permit for one of those units, and made the trip mostly because I simply love the country and had not planned another hunt in its place. Plus, I was curious to see how badly the herd had been decimated. In my mind, with 50 percent of the antelope herd lost in the region, it was going to be like walking into a ghost town. I was surprised to discover that nothing was further from the truth.

Antelope still seemed to be everywhere I looked. Maybe the herds weren't quite as large, but there were large numbers of antelope. This only told me that, due to three or four very mild winters, the antelope herd in that area had grown beyond the reasonable carrying capacity of the range. And I was surprised to see that most of the bucks were amazingly very large. During the first 2 days of hunting, I glassed at least eight or nine different bucks pushing 15 inches.

The third morning, I made my move on a fine 15-inch buck with good paddles, and slipped to within 200 yards. That pronghorn never knew what hit him as I squeezed off a shot with my favored 7mm Rem. Magnum Ruger Model 77.

I was still reveling in my great shooting as I crossed the draw between me and my downed trophy. As I approached the corner of a woven-wire fence line, I was immediately sickened by the sight before me. Lying there, shrivelled in the sun, were the dehydrated carcasses of more than 150 pronghorns that had not survived the winter. Not even the coyotes, eagles, ravens and magpies had been able to fully utilize the loss. At that moment, the elation of a great stalk and good shooting were suddenly overshadowed by the thought that I'd just shot a survivor of one of the worst winters in Wyoming wildlife history. It wasn't a good feeling.

- Toby Bridges

Large herd of pronghorns on their winter range

Social Interaction

TERRITORIES. Where the elements do not threaten pronghorn survival during the winter months, they may remain in well-established home territories throughout the entire year. However, where or when winters are more severe, antelope readily congregate in large herds, often numbering a thousand or more animals. These huge concentrations may be made up of 50 or more smaller bands, many of which may have once competed for the same territory. However, with the onslaught of a harsh winter and deep snows, the bands must come together to find habitat with adequate winter forage, water and protection from the elements.

Where antelope must migrate from their familiar home territory to a winter range, the round trip may require a journey of over 100 miles. As spring approaches, large winter groups begin to break up as smaller herds return to their home areas. The does give birth to their fawns once the animals reach their home territory.

The breakup of winter herds commonly begins in March across much of the antelope's northern range. Almost as soon as the snow melts and new vegetation emerges, dominant bucks begin selecting and establishing home territories with excellent habitat within the boundaries. Does and yearling fawns join the dominant buck in his territory, forming a temporary herd unit.

Each dominant buck selects and marks the boundaries of an area that contains elements of suitable habitat, including breaks, ridges and open country. The territory must include good forage and a nearby water source.

The selection of ideal habitat within a territory helps bring does into the buck's realm. The number drawn may not be particularly significant to the buck until the rut approaches, when does and fawns move from one defended territory to another as they wish.

A dominant buck does not become possessive of "his" does until the pre-rut. Then, he will try his best to detain as many does as possible within his territory. This is the beginning of a considerable management problem for the herd buck as the rut proceeds. He will aggressively defend his piece of real estate against the intrusion of other bucks, often well after the end of the rut in late fall.

During the brief birthing period in the spring, does will run off their yearling offspring, leave the herd and bear their young. As soon as the newborn fawns are able to follow and graze with the mother, she rejoins the herd. While yearlings are beginning to enter adulthood, it is not uncommon for them to rejoin their mother doe and her new fawns once they move back into the herd.

From spring through late summer, the herd within a dominant buck's domain establishes normal daily routines of feeding, resting and moving to water. Barring any major changes in the environment, such as an extended period of drought, which can alter the supply of food and water, this pattern of daily movement remains fairly constant until the rutting period approaches. Does and their fawns can enjoy a relatively hassle-free spring and summer in any buck's defended territory.

Like most young animals, antelope fawns romp, run and play, exercising and developing their strong leg muscles. However, among antelope these characteristics

THE FLAGGING TECHNIQUE was developed by the Plains Indians. In this 1832-1833 painting by George Catlin, an Indian has attracted a curious pronghorn herd from a long distance by simply attaching a colored piece of cloth to a stick and letting the "flag" blow in the wind. (Provided by the Smithsonian American Art museum, Washington D.C./Art Resource, NY.)

are not displayed by only the young. The same antics are also part of adult behavior. It's not uncommon to watch a lone adult make a headlong run or charge at the rest of a group or herd. This often precipitates a run and chase melee that may be joined by the entire herd. The high-speed running, quick turns, fake attacks, and circular movements appear to be enjoyed by all participants.

SOCIAL ORDER. Among most herd animals there is a pecking order, and pronghorns are no exception. Playful sparring between fawns begins at an early age. While these early bouts are more play than serious challenge, they serve as the beginning of established dominance. Groups or herds of does and yearlings establish this pecking order through assertiveness. Once settled, the ranking of individuals stays relatively stable until a major change forces a restructure of dominance, which could be due to the loss of a dominant doe, the merging of several doe groups or even a change in the dominant buck. While the dominant buck may command the territory he has marked, it is the dominant doe that usually has charge of the does and yearlings. Establishing and maintaining the adult doe and fawn/yearling rank status with minimum challenge is key to keeping chaos to a minimum and ensuring peace and stability within the group.

Antelope bucks tend to be more unsettled than does. Their challenges as fawns continue into adulthood, with the biggest, strongest and more aggressive bucks eventually becoming the masters of a territory. Within groups of bachelor bucks that inhabit territory not claimed by a dominant buck, the pecking order is frequently tested. Those bachelor bucks that prove themselves by ousting a herd buck thus earn the reward

of herd buck status. However, during hunting season, the graduation from satellite buck to herd buck often occurs with a single gunshot. When this happens, challenges and counter-challenges among the bucks are waged. In the end, the toughest guy in the valley takes over the territory.

PERSONALITY. When it comes to winning the "most curious" big-game title, the pronghorn is the undisputed champion. Unusual things that move immediately catch an antelope's attention. Thanks to their fantastic eyesight and the open habitat in which they live, pronghorns are quick to pick up on anything that's different, anything that's out of place. A piece of paper blowing across the open prairie or flapping in a strong breeze can hold a pronghorn's attention for hours.

Since mobility is not a problem for pronghorns, they'll often travel considerable distances just to check something out to satisfy their curiosity. A sight that would send a whitetail deer into instant panic and flight merely draws the attention of antelope, which typically flee only after they feel threatened by the unexpected appearance of something unusual.

Insatiable curiosity has proven to be the downfall of many individual pronghorns. The irresistible urge to investigate things they can't readily identify has lured many antelope within a hunter's shooting range. Plains Indians found they could tie a piece of light-colored cloth or buckskin on a stick, then wave it just above the horizon or the top of tall grass and brush where a distant pronghorn would catch the movement and take interest. Many times the curious animal would approach to within range of their primitive weapons. Today's hunters still successfully use

Two pronghorn bucks fighting over a doe in estrus

this "flagging" method. A hat, handkerchief or other visible object waved back and forth a few times just above enough cover to hide the hunter often draws animals that haven't been overly pressured. Throughout much of the pronghorn range, this tactic works as well today as it did 200 years ago.

Nervous, wired and alert, pronghorns seem to always be in a state of continual motion. Other than when bedded, a herd seldom remains motionless for any length of time. And even the bedding periods are usually short. Always on edge, antelope continually scan their territory, relying on their keen eyesight to monitor everything around them. While the animals may be curious enough to approach and check out an unknown object or movement, they instantly flee from anything perceived as danger.

The hierarchy of a herd can vary from group to group, but in most the oldest doe is the primary lookout and the most wary animal. Often an old, dominant doe is actually the herd leader, even when a dominant buck is present. Timid and cautious, a pronghorn herd closely monitors the movement of predators such as coyotes, avoiding them and giving them a wide berth when on the move. However, does have been observed savagely defending themselves or their young against predators like coyotes and bobcats, using sharp front hooves to strike out at the intruder.

As wary and cautious as pronghorns can be, they also have a high tolerance for familiar things. In cattle country, for example, they see pickup trucks and other vehicles in their territory almost constantly as ranchers tend livestock, check water sources, mend fences and perform other daily ranch duties. Pickups and horse-mounted riders become a part of the pronghorn's daily life, and they learn to accept them. But a human on foot is not normal and likely won't be trusted.

Pronghorns don't seem to mind the presence of a moving vehicle, even at close range. Many times they'll race a moving vehicle if it suits their fancy. However, during the hunting seasons they quickly learn that vehicles mean danger. And while they may continue to tolerate moving vehicles during the season, they learn that the shooting doesn't start until the vehicle stops. To fool these pronghorn, some hunters use a tactic that involves having a hunter bail out of the vehicle as it slowly moves past good cover. The hunter then remains hidden as the vehicle slowly eases on across the plains or down the dusty two-track. As often as not, a pronghorn stands there and watches the vehicle as it moves off, giving the hunter an easy shot. Before ever beginning a stalk on distant pronghorns, the smart hunter always parks his vehicle out of sight.

Pronghorns are tremendous horizontal jumpers. But after some 20 million years of evolution, they still have not caught on to jumping vertically. While long leaps of 25 feet or more are not uncommon for antelope running at 50 mph, rarely do they jump a strand of barbed wire 3 to 4 feet high. However, they physically are perfectly capable of jumping over fences, and some will. Most, though, choose instead to crawl under a fence or through the strands of a barbed-wire fence. A common, very patternable trait of pronghorns is to cross under a fence at the same spot each time. This tendency is so strong that they may run several miles along a fence line to get to their favorite crossing spot.

Fences, especially of the woven wire variety, are formidable barriers that continue to impact herd numbers in many areas. Any fence that cannot be crossed under or through shuts off pronghorns from potentially suitable habitat.

COMMUNICATION. Pronghorn vocalization is not well understood. Since biologists and hunting experts are just now beginning to identify the different sounds made by antelope, considerable research is still needed on the subject. While a number of different sounds (calls) can be attributed to the pronghorn, just what they mean or how they are interpreted by other antelope remains to be determined. For example, the bleat of a fawn could bring the mother doe running, or she could simply respond with a bleat of her own. Likewise, when an injured or wounded buck emits a loud bawl, it could bring another buck charging in with its mane standing straight up, ready for a scrap. Or, the very same sound could send another buck high-tailing it over a distant ridge top.

Both sexes give out a sharp, raspy snort or bark. Often this single bark is given as an alarm, but animals have also been observed making this sound as they are feeding and not at all in an aroused state. When challenging an adversary, a buck generally makes a snort-chuckle noise that sounds like "blat-ta-ta-ta-ta-ta." The accepted interpretation is, "I'm here and ready to fight."

The challenge call is common throughout the rutting period as bachelor bucks try to encroach upon the territory of herd bucks in their attempt to steal does. The use of this call is a new technique for hunting pronghorns. In fact, until recent years, these sounds were thought to be bird noises. Now Mel Dutton, manufacturer of the Dutton antelope decoy, and Brad Harris, of Lohman Calls, have teamed up to develop an antelope challenge call, representing a major breakthrough for pronghorn hunters. During the rut, some bowhunters are discovering that challenge calling combined with decoying is an extremely effective technique for taking pronghorn bucks.

Probably the best known communication used by antelope is the flash of the white hairs on the rump. When aroused or frightened, pronghorns extend the long, white guard hairs of the rump patch, creating a bright, white flash that can be seen by other pronghorns for long distances. It serves as a warning to other antelope, and is generally followed by headlong flight.

COHABITATION. Pronghorns can live in harmony sharing the same habitat with cattle and horses. Although they may keep a noticeable distance

The Exception to the Rule

Several years ago I was hunting a ranch along the Niobrara River in eastern Wyoming. There was a small herd of antelope living in a large pasture behind the barn. When we went out in the pickup to hunt each morning, they would vacate the pasture. No matter where they were in that pasture, the herd would run to the fence and crawl under it at one specific spot. There wasn't anything different about the fence in this spot. It was just their spot.

The herd buck wasn't exactly a shooter, but we were still interested in observing him because he was a confirmed fence-jumper. He would run along the fence with the does and yearlings, then while they were scurrying under the fence, he would effortlessly jump over it. Having read several times that pronghorns absolutely don't jump fences, I was taken aback the first time I saw the buck jump it. Having a good vertical leap, he easily cleared it with room to spare.

For 3 days in a row, the herd left the pasture as we approached. Without fail, the does and yearlings crossed under at exactly the same place. And even when we pressured the buck a bit, he would jump the fence between the same two fence posts. Antelope logic being as it is, it may have been the only place he thought he could jump the wires, just as the others would only crawl under at one specific place.

- Don Oster

between themselves and domestic stock, the stock's presence doesn't appear to be a problem. Mule deer also commonly share much of the same habitat where pronghorns live, and while the two species generally maintain some separation, they are regularly seen feeding in the same hay field at the same time. The animal that antelope don't care to have as close neighbors are sheep. Normally the sharing of pasture goes like this: sheep in, pronghorns out.

AN ALARMED PRONGHORN (arrow) will flare the white hairs on its rump to alert other animals that danger is nearby.

Ol' Susie

This looked like the perfect setup to collect a super trophy antelope. The sight through the binoculars has been permanently burned into my memory. Backlit on the skyline in the early morning's glow were two 16-inch-plus bucks standing horn-to-horn, with a passel of does grazing indifferently nearby. Both sets of horns looked very big, even from over 600 yards away. Without a doubt, they were both shooters.

The two were trying to settle their differences over the right to breed those does right then and there while the prizes grazed as if totally unconcerned with the proceedings. Each one was determined to make the other vacate the premises, leaving the twenty or so ladies to himself. Both bucks were completely unaware of our presence and

would be very approachable. We patiently watched them fight, figuring the herd would slowly move over the nearby rise, presenting the perfect opportunity for us to stalk within range where I could take my pick of the two massive bucks.

Well, the stalk didn't go according to plan. You see, one doe in the group didn't like pickup trucks at any distance. She quit grazing to study us for a while, then moved off down the ridge in a gallop. Almost as soon as the first doe started moving, the others chose to follow. The fight came to an immediate stop as the two magnificent bucks scampered after the herd of does. Since the girls had been the reason for the fight, they weren't about to let them get away. They would continue the confrontation at a different time and different place. The destination of the herd? Who knows; they ran across at least three ridges and out of sight. Try as we did, we never saw them again during the hunt. Now it was clear that my least favorite prong-horn, the dominant doe, or as I like to say, Ol' Susie, had struck again.

In most states, antelope season coincides with the rut. This time of year finds herd bucks in a constant state of confusion. Among their many jobs are checking the harem for signs of estrus, performing the breeding, whipping or warding off all intruding bucks, while constantly herding to keep the does under some semblance of control. Simultaneously wearing all these hats can make the buck just too busy to pay much attention to the presence of hunters or other potential signs of danger. In that sense, he takes on the role of a follower, not the true herd leader.

In every herd there is one dominant old doe, the one I like to call Susie. From all observations, she's the antelope that appears to be running the show, generally playing havoc with hunter attempts to stalk the herd buck. Nobody wants to shoot the old bat, except maybe out of frustration, but she doesn't know that. Many experienced pronghorn hunters claim the Susie in any herd is an old dry doe that takes on a matriarchal position at the top of the doe pecking order. Dry or not, she is always a nibby, unforgiving old doe. She's always poking her nose into what's going on in the area, and almost nothing escapes her scrutiny. More than the other does, Ol' Susie has her head up constantly, always scanning the terrain with her built-in binoculars, looking for anything that might represent a threat to the herd. When she barks, every antelope in the herd listens.

Now, this doesn't mean that all the other antelope in a herd are oblivious. When a hunter is faced with making a stalk on a herd with 6, 12 or 18 or more sets of those big, watchful doe eyes, he has his work cut out for him, even without Susie's intuitive inclinations. Her attention immediately focuses on any movement or strange occurrence spotted by any member of the band. She will closely inspect for herself and decide for all what can be ignored. If Susie's nosy disposition proves irritating, her jumpiness can be downright maddening. She will spook at the slightest provocation, be it the sight of a far-off pickup truck, a hunter on foot, a car that stops along a distant road or any of many other routine occurrences. When she goes, the rest follow. You can always spot Susie easily. She's the first to run, then she takes the lead as the troupe heads toward the next county. The buck, being preoccupied, just goes along with the herd. Often he'll lag behind the others, and stop out of curiosity to take a last look. But there is no way he'll let the does get too far ahead.

Distance and travel are always on the pronghorn's itinerary. In their ground-covering gallop, they can quickly cover several miles. Susie normally stops once there is some distance, and a barrier such as a hill or ridge, between her and the perceived danger. She appears to practice the "out of sight, out of danger" doctrine. Once the does settled down, the buck, wearing his many hats, again tries to take control. That is, until something spooks Ol' Susie again.

On a hunt in eastern Wyoming a couple of years ago, I watched a buck actually take charge away from Susie, if only for a few moments. We were watching from a distance and apparently weren't far enough away to suit Susie. She was nervous, and kept edging out away from the herd, trying to lead them up a nearby draw. There were a couple of satellite bucks in that draw and the herd buck didn't want his private stock near them. He kept circling to the side of the group, herding them away from the draw. Susie continued her little breakaway tactic several times, and each time the buck hazed her back with the rest of the does.

Finally, it became apparent that the buck had had it with her obstinate behavior. The next time she sidled toward the draw, he quickly charged at her, headed her off, circled and gave her a good hard horn hook in the rear, sending her contrary butt back to join the others. She promptly moved through the herd and trotted away in a different direction, leading the rest away. Unable to head them off, the buck merely followed.

Pronghorns, in their open-country habitat, seem to establish a comfortable distance between themselves and potential hazards. Because they can usually see most of the activity around them, they won't be bothered by things at or beyond that distance. Prior to the hunting seasons, this comfort zone can be relatively small, and while the animals never lose their curiosity or wariness, they become almost approachable. Many acquaintances, upon returning from a western vacation, tell me that it must be awfully easy to shoot an antelope. They see hundreds near the highway, grazing like so many cows. Of course, none have ever tried one of these "easy" hunts.

The comfort or safety zone widens when the hunting season opens. Many early-season pronghorns are taken at reasonable range from a rest across the hood of a truck. While legal in most states as long as the vehicle is not on a public roadway, it's not exactly pronghorn hunting. Pickup trucks, which the pronghorns see continuously during the year as ranchers check cattle, run fences or check water supplies, are usually ignored until the season starts. Vehicles bring hunters, and the goats are quick studies. They learn quickly that a moving vehicle poses little threat. The instant it stops, however, the antelope shift into high gear. The more a herd is buggered or chased, or stalked and shot at, the larger the comfort zone gets until almost anything sends them into flight.

In most cases, the biggest group of does are accompanied by the biggest buck in the area. However, one of the best trophy collection opportunities occurs when an old buck goes it alone. It may be because he has been whipped by a more aggressive buck, or has quit the does temporarily because of hunting pressure. Some old herd bucks cut out on their own when hunters persist in following and bothering a herd. They won't let the does get totally away and they will rejoin the group in due time. These old loners, some of them big in horns and not accompanied by Susie and the girls, are a trophy hunter's dream. Always carefully look over a lone buck. The buster of your dreams may be the one standing out on the prairie all by himself. Generally speaking, pronghorn bucks don't appear to be particularly wary when separated from their doe support group. Loners are approachable, and while not exactly totally vulnerable, they are good candidates for a successful stalk.

- Don Oster

Movement

Early naturalists to visit the American West regularly witnessed the relationship between the pronghorn and the huge herds of buffalo. However, they left little documentation of just how much the movement of the great buffalo herds – which typically numbered into the thousands – affected the movement of the pronghorn. But there is no doubt that the pronghorn benefited from its relationship with the great shaggy beasts, especially during the winter months, when a buffalo could open wide areas of snow-covered ground by swinging its massive head back and forth. Even rock-hard, crusted snow caps were easily broken through by the buffalo's powerful front legs and hooves. Following in the wake of a buffalo herd, antelope could easily find plenty to eat. The buffalo kept travel routes to water sources open as well.

While pronghorn movement patterns during the mid-1800s were not recorded, the annual migrations of some buffalo herds were identified. Many of the northern herds would move between 200 and 400 miles from preferred summer range to winter range which better met their needs through the cold months. Did the herds of pronghorns that moved with them travel the full distance of these migrations, or were they residents of a smaller geographical, and only joining the buffalo migration for a short period, then staying behind as resident antelope from a new area took their place? This is a part of the pronghorn puzzle that will likely never be fully known. The days of buffalo and pronghorns sharing the same range in significant numbers were long past by the time modern game management practices were established.

Antelope are highly mobile animals, physically able to move long distances with relative ease. Historically, the animals could range totally free across the sweeping, wide-open plains to seek any habitat that suited them. Just how far they would move before the influences of 20th century man remains a mystery. Everywhere in today's range, free movement has been inhibited by

barriers. Now, natural barriers are an impediment to pronghorn range expansion. These include heavy forests, large rivers, deep canyons, mountains or badlands. To these, man has added a number of other obstacles; namely woven-wire fences, interstate highways, roadways, canals and railroads. These encroachments on pronghorn range have seriously impacted antelope movement. Many experts feel that the pronghorn once roamed widely, maybe as widely as the buffalo, with summer and winter range separated by hundreds of miles.

Today's pronghorn is, in one respect, a completely different animal than its ancestors that once had full range of the West. Today's antelope has adapted to man's use of the land. Instead of migrating between summer and winter range, most have learned to fully utilize the most accessible resources. Where good forage and water exist, pronghorns may not need to change locations at all through the entire year, and many live out their lives within a relatively small area.

SEASONAL MOVEMENT

Antelope migrate only based on the availability of forage and water. The biggest natural threats to

pronghorn survival, and those that can necessitate movement to a new location, are deep snow and drought. Today, roughly 80 percent of the North American antelope population lives in what can be considered "good" habitat, with adequate forage and water supplies. Ruling out severe winter snows or prolonged dry conditions, most of these antelope rarely move more than 5 to 10 miles within their range during the entire year. Where range conditions are optimal, with sufficient forage and water, a group may be content to spend its entire life within one large pasture. And even when a number of smaller bands gather into a large winter herd, during most years movement is minimal, as long as there is an adequate supply of food and water. However, a study in Wyoming has revealed that some bucks tend to be wanderers, especially during the rut period, and break from the norm by covering a much larger area.

When and where winter weather or drought conditions persist, antelope move a considerable distance to find more favorable habitat. Unfortunately, emergency moves often have a tragic ending, such as the attempted migration by about 150 antelope in eastern Wyoming a few years ago. To escape the ravages of a severe blizzard crippling the area, the pronghorns found easy walking on a cleared railroad track and began following it in the direction of the Black Hills. Along the way, they encountered a major obstacle that threw them a real curve. They came upon a highway bridge that crossed over the top of the open tracks. The herd would not walk under the bridge, thereby ending their journey. Although they had nearly reached their winter destination, which offered accessible food and water, the animals turned around and tried returning to their original home area. Nearly all of the herd was lost to the cold and starvation. Blizzards of that magnitude were unusual for that particular area, and those pronghorns were unaccustomed to making a major migration. That they even tried to find food and water sources outside of where they had lived their entire lives is a credit to their amazing survival instincts.

Pronghorn herds inhabiting mountain foothills or high country commonly move into lower valleys during the winter to escape snows that cover food supplies and threaten survival. Unlike the true migration of caribou from annual summer to winter ranges, with predetermined beginning and ending locations, the distance of the pronghorns' seasonal movement is directly related to snow depth and availability of food and water. Where antelope are known to live in high country of 8,000 to 9,000 feet, it's not uncommon for them to travel 50 or more miles to find food. The necessary altitude adjustments become an annual part of the high-country dweller's life cycle, with the herd returning to its home range as soon as the snows melt.

DAILY MOVEMENT

Three primary factors determine an antelope's range and the distance of daily herd movement within the seasons: the availability and proximity of forage and water; barriers that restrict or funnel movement; and the amount of disturbance, such as hunting pressure.

As a general rule, antelope go to water at least once a day. During spring and summer, when food and water tend to be more readily available, a herd may move no more than a mile or so within its home range as long as its members are not disturbed. Any physical barriers to their movement are adapted to as long as they do not block access to needed resources. In fall and winter, when food resources change, daily herd movement to search for forage and water covers as many miles as necessary. This need to expand the range to reach forage can be complicated by the presence of barriers, which may cause a herd to adapt to a different feeding area or water hole. Once a herd is established in an area, their daily pattern of bedding, feeding and watering remains fairly constant until another change in available resources occurs.

The hunter who spends several days scouting an area from a distance can easily discern the daily movement pattern of the pronghorns in the area. Much like whitetail deer, pronghorns exhibit a regular movement pattern when not disturbed. Watching their daily routine from a distance through a good set of binoculars or spotting scope, a hunter can size up the bucks within the hunt area, determine feeding and watering patterns, and establish the best places to set up an ambush. Bowhunters and hunters armed with traditional-styled muzzleloaders often find that the only successful way to get within close range of a wary pronghorn is ambushing it from a blind strategically located near a water hole, along a well-used travel route, or near a fence cross-under that a herd habitually uses. Knowing the daily movement pattern of antelope within an area also allows the hunter who prefers calling and decoying to move into place long before the antelope are within sight.

Hunting pressure often alters daily antelope movement patterns, and after a few close brushes with hunters or hunters' vehicles in the area, the naturally nervous pronghorn becomes even more skittish. Early in the season, antelope are generally approachable by a hunter making a carefully planned stalk. However, even if they're spooked by a hunter on foot, rarely will they blow completely out of the country. As often as not, the herd regularly runs over the next ridge or rise and out of sight of whatever caused them to run, where the pronghorns quickly settle down and begin grazing or resting. Lightly hunted antelope remain in their general territory, moving about with their accustomed daily pattern.

Heavy hunting pressure drastically alters their behavior and daily movements. Where antelope have been heavily hunted and chased, they may take instant flight at the first sight of a person or vehicle, frantically racing for several miles before stopping. When and where hunting pressure becomes really excessive, pronghorns seek out the roughest country, heavy cover or deep draws to escape human contact. If they find sufficient forage and food in their sanctuary, a pressured herd may stay there until the season's end.

Hunting pronghorns on public ground, such as lands controlled by the Bureau of Land Management or large tracts of national grassland, can become hard work. Other hunters have as much right to be there as you do, making it impossible to have the area all to yourself. However, when faced with hunting public

Pronghorn Sanctuary

A couple of years ago, my son and I were hunting on a ranch in eastern Montana. This particular area had been hunted fairly hard in the early part of the season, but there were still some remaining scattered bands of pronghorns on the property.

I was lucky enough to shoot a good 15-inch buck the first day. However, the sound of my shot triggered what looked like a mass antelope exodus over the horizon. The next morning, there was nary a hide nor hair to be seen. I broke out a topo map and we discovered a large, camel-hump-shaped hill about 2 miles east of the last road on the property. The map showed no marked roads or two-trackers for at least another 2 miles beyond the hump.

We dismounted the truck and started walking across the prairie, wondering what lay hidden beyond the hill.

When we reached the top of the steep hump, a careful look on the other side revealed a hidden valley nearly a mile across. From our perch, we counted almost 50 antelope in small herds peacefully grazing toward a pond at the head of the valley. And best of all, there were several very nice bucks mixed in the groups.

I'd like to report that we stalked into range and my son nailed a big buck. Unfortunately, the valley was across the property line where no hunting was allowed. We had found a sanctuary for all of the pressured antelope in the area and you could bet they wouldn't go back to their old territory until the hunting season was well over.

- Don Oster

areas, the hunter who does not mind putting in a little extra effort can usually still enjoy a successful hunt.

If herds seem to disappear once they have been heavily pressured, the solution may be just over that distant ridge, away from vehicle access. This is where updated topographical maps are worth their weight in gold. They allow you to locate places in your hunting area which may not be accessed by two-track vehicle trails. When the pronghorns no longer lounge around out in the open, it's time to get out and do some walking. And in the big country the pronghorn calls home, this can mean getting a lot of exercise. But the cautious hunter who approaches remote draws, valleys and other secluded hideaways may find a concentration of antelope living peaceably where others hunters haven't yet been due to the fact that the location is not easily reached by vehicle.

Hunting pressure can work in your favor just as well as it works against you. A boundary fence-line may mark the property lines of neighboring ranches, and often the boundary of one's hunting area, but the antelope that make the area home have absolutely no problem crossing under to the other side, especially when hard pressed by hunters. More than one successful pronghorn hunter owes the trophy he took to the fact that a barrage of ill-placed long-range shots on a neighboring ranch sent a buck or two scurrying onto the land they were hunting. Even when pushed, pronghorns tend to utilize fence crossings that are a part of their daily movement routine, and these are a great place to intercept bucks pushed from adjacent range by hunting pressure.

A Pronghorn Promise

Most outdoor writers seem to live by the motto, "I do what I do, so I can do what I do." It's a way of life that's not bad if you don't mind living from article check to article check, driving a well-used four-wheel-drive pickup, staying at hole-in-the-wall motels, eating fast food on the go and spending lots of time away from the family. But the hunting's great!

Fellow outdoor writer Jim Shockey had been gone from home for more than a month when I picked him up at the Sheridan, Wyoming airport a few seasons back. Jim had flown straight to Wyoming from a combination moose and caribou hunt in northern British Columbia to hunt pronghorns with me. That fall I was guiding hunts for Lone Wolf Outfitters (Buffalo, WY) and had successfully filled out several hunters on the ranch where I planned to take Jim.

This was his first pronghorn hunt and he really wanted to take a good buck, one that would qualify for the muzzleloading big-game record book. With that in mind, I had purposely kept my other hunters away from a huge, several-hundred acre hay field nearly in the center of the ranch. I had left it as something of a refuge, and knew of at least three near-15-inch horned bucks that had moved into the area due to surrounding hunting pressure.

As we drove out to the ranch the next morning in the pre-dawn darkness, Jim confessed to me that he really needed to get home. He had been gone just too long, and besides being behind on a few writing assignments, he missed his family. Although we had scheduled 3 days for his hunt, he wanted to know if it could be accomplished any sooner.

"Take the first buck that I say tops the minimum score of 63 points, and I'll have you on a plane home tomorrow," I promised him.

In the dark, I nosed my pickup off the road so we could watch the hay field come daybreak. In the first light, two shooter bucks with a group of about 12 pronghorn does worked into the field. Either buck would have scored in the upper 60s or low 70s. I backed out and drove up the road a mile, then pulled off. Jim grabbed his .50 caliber Knight DISC Rifle, and we eased up over a grassy knoll to look in the small valley on the other side. A fine 15-inch buck with good prongs stood watching over a small band of does. Jim crawled another 200 yards through the knee-high grass, then made a great 170-yard sitting shot. We had been out of the truck less than 15 minutes, and he had his muzzleloading record book pronghorn.

That buck scored about 75 Boone and Crockett points, and my hunting partner was on his way home the next day.

- Toby Bridges

Jim Shockey and his record book buck

Herd buck with his harem

The Pronghorn Rut

In areas where mature does far outnumber mature bucks, many adult does do not get bred on an annual basis. Unlike the whitetail doe, pronghorn does come into estrus just once, and for a relatively short period. Throughout most of North America, the whitetail doe comes into her estrus period some-time in November (although earlier October estrus periods have taken place), and where the buck-to-doe ratio is not too far out of balance, the vast majority of does are bred. However, if a whitetail doe fails to conceive or is not bred at all during this period, she will enter her second estrus period 28 days later. And if she is not bred then, she will enter estrus again for a third and, if necessary, fourth time, each 28 days later than the last period. Consequently, nearly all whitetail does are bred over a rut period that may last 4 or more months.

Not so with pronghorn does. The pronghorn rut is something of a one-shot affair, for the does anyway. In the northernmost antelope range of southern Canada, the rut can kick in as early as late August, and in the southernmost climes the rut can take place as late as early November. However, throughout

most central western states, the pronghorn rut is in full swing from about the middle of September to mid-October. And when does begin to enter estrus, the entire rut for a specific geographical area lasts only about 2 weeks.

Preceding the actual rut, the amiable social structure of an antelope herd begins to break down. The now nearly grown fawns generally remain with the herd, but begin to ignore the social structure established among the mature animals. Doe fawns stick close to mother does, while the young-of-the-year buck fawns begin hanging out together, mimicking the antics of adult bucks.

As the rut commences, dominant bucks often become intolerant of any other buck in the herd. At this time, there are two distinct buck groups: the dominant bucks, which have established territories, and the bachelor bucks, which roam real estate not claimed by a dominant buck. When a bachelor buck wanders into the territory of a dominant buck, a fierce battle can result.

A fitting description for a bachelor buck is "sexually motivated marauder." Bucks living in unclaimed territory and trespassing into the territories of other bucks will try all means possible to steal and breed does wherever they find them.

Pronghorn bucks less than 3 to 4 years of age usually do not have the opportunity to breed. The dominant bucks that establish harems of 15 to 20 does are the

upon these territory markers deposit their scent in the same manner.

Similar to a whitetail buck, pronghorn bucks establish scrapes by pawing out a small barren spot on the ground. In the making of the scrape, pronghorns deposit scent from between their front hooves. And like deer, they also regularly rub vegetation with their forehead, again depositing scent that identifies ownership of the territory. In short, the pronghorn buck posts several different types of "no trespassing" signs along the perimeter of what he has established as his domain.

The entire process of establishing and marking territory, defending it against intruders, and gathering does is all about breeding and reproduction. For the week or so prior to the beginning of the rut, then during the actual rut when breeding takes place, the herd buck is one very busy fellow. Not only will he defend his harem from the challenges of rival bucks, but he also breeds every doe that accepts him. However, in reality it is the doe selecting the buck. Most biologists believe that the doe's selection probably occurs before the rut and is indicated by her willingness to remain within a specific buck's territory. During the course of her lifetime, a pronghorn doe normally gives birth no more than six times, even though she becomes sexually mature during her second year and can live to be 10 years of age.

The dominant buck must always be on guard for other bucks, who are seemingly always present, wanting to challenge for possession of does gathered for the purpose of breeding. And if that's not enough to keep

ones doing 90 percent or more of all breeding. Until a buck reaches maturity and the size to become a dominant buck with a band of does all to himself, the subordinate male has very little interaction with does during the rut, especially during the doe estrus period.

As the rut nears, mature bucks often exhibit a behavior that is often referred to as "pronghorn crazy." During this period, the bucks exhibit a wide range of bizarre antics, some of which cause pronghorn biologists and experts to scratch their heads and wonder, "Why?" It's not unusual to see a buck leaping around and shaking its head back and forth from side to side, like a bucking bronc, then minutes later stand listless, with its head down. For no apparent reason, bucks often twitch body muscles to make the body hair ripple, or frequently flare the white rump patch. Many bucks run in a tight circle, occasionally making sideways leaps. While such pre-rut behavior generally attracts the attention or curiosity of other nearby antelope, it seems to serve no real purpose other than to interest a doe.

Dominant, or herd bucks, mark the territories they establish. One of the most common markers, and the one that is most visible to the hunter scouting an area, is piles of droppings that can usually be found along the boundary between the territories of two or more bucks. Often these piles cover an area nearly 10 feet square, indicating that more than one buck has been urinating and depositing feces in the same spot on a regular basis. Bachelor bucks that happen

Buck making a scrape

49

him busy, the does also often have minds of their own and don't always agree to go where he wants. The buck is constantly herding, urging and trying to control them, while still continually checking them for signs of the upcoming estrus period. Then, there is the actual breeding when a receptive doe accepts him. And all this while keeping the lookout for other bucks ready to steal all or part of his harem.

RIVAL BUCKS often try to steal a doe from the herd buck's harem.

All is Fair in Love and War!

While on a muzzleloading elk hunt in the Gallo Mountains of western New Mexico (near the Arizona border) my hunting partner and I were making a short drive through a stretch of high plains to a new hunting area when we topped a slight rise and spotted a beautiful 16-inch trophy antelope with a harem of about a dozen does. The herd was only about 200 yards from the road, and we stopped to take a better look at the Boone-and-Crockett class pronghorn through our binoculars.

We had barely stopped when two younger, 14-inch bucks appeared on a ridge several hundred yards behind the herd. One of the bucks ran down toward the herd, then skirted off a hundred yards to one side. The advance was more than the herd buck could tolerate, and in a flash the race was on. Both bucks disappeared over the distant horizon several miles away, and each time they topped a new rise, the bigger buck was hooking the younger buck in the rump with his tall horns.

The pair had barely disappeared when the second 14-inch buck ran down, rounded up the small herd of does and ran them around a nearby butte and out of sight. As we pulled away, my partner commented, "I'll bet those two switch off and pull that trick every day!"

- Toby Bridges

When an intruder finally gets brazen enough to cross into another buck's territory, the herd buck commonly begins his defense by first attempting to stare down the challenger. If the confrontation escalates beyond this, the dominant buck's next defensive step is to approach his antagonist with a very stiff-legged walk, snorting repeatedly. It's mostly show, and to try intimidating his opponent, the defending herd buck generally extends the hair on the back of his neck to make himself look bigger and more overpowering. As he moves slowly toward the intruder, the herd buck also postures, allowing him to show off his horns, which he will shake menacingly at his rival. Normally, most bachelor bucks are smaller, less mature pronghorns and the herd buck's larger size, bigger horns and aggressive display is nearly always enough to cause his challenger to turn and high-tail it over the next ridge.

Rarely is there an outright clash between the two. The few fights that do break out are usually fast, short-lived affairs. A dominant buck's quick headlong charge more often than not results in the challenger's hasty retreat, and the extent of the contact usually amounts to little more than the hook of a horn in the rump of the departing pronghorn.

This isn't to say that real fights don't take place. Where pronghorn densities are fairly high, a dominant herd buck may be faced by two, three, four or even more challengers each day during the rut. It's inevitable that sooner or later a confrontation results in solid horn-to-horn contact. These battles can be extremely fierce as the two bucks slash out at each other with the hooks and prongs of their horns, along

FIGHTS between bucks sometimes end with the winner jabbing his horns into the side of the loser. The buck above, which has a large amount of hair stuck to his horns, was no doubt victorious over his challenger.

with their sharp front hooves. By rut's end, plenty of bucks carry battle scars on their shoulders and chest. Even so, serious injuries from fights are rare.

Things get really interesting when a pair of bachelor bucks team up to work a dominant buck. It's nearly impossible for a herd buck to keep up with more than one opponent. While he's busy running one away from his does, the other quickly runs in and tries to steal or breed some does. Often, the herd buck does not pursue very far, and will return immediately to ward off the advances of the other buck. However, repeated attempts by a pair of bachelor bucks can run the dominant buck to exhaustion, making each of their new attempts easier. A herd buck assembling an unusually large harem attracts a great deal of attention from bachelor bucks. And when more than two begin to make their raids, it becomes increasingly difficult for the dominant buck to maintain control of his herd, especially if some of the does attempt to willingly leave with their new suitors.

The territories established by dominant bucks work to the advantage of a pronghorn herd in general. When a buck selects and marks his territory, it is typically good habitat with sufficient forage and water, which ensures the health of the does and their fawns. Despite all the advances from subordinate bachelor bucks, the dominant herd buck does most or all of the breeding, passing on his healthy, aggressive genes. Inside a buck's territory, protection of the does by the dominant buck eliminates the pressure of the does being continually pursued by numerous bucks throughout the entire rut. It also provides a haven for bearing and rearing the young. Although does may leave the defended territory of one buck, as a rule they simply move into another buck's domain.

With so many bucks competing for the does, it's obvious that the ownership of a territory can quickly change. An older buck slightly past his prime may be able to withstand the rigors of the rut at the outset, and handle all the breeding and herd protection responsibilities. However, when a younger, healthier buck of nearly the same size comes along, the sheer stamina of the newcomer can result in a hand-over of territorial power, and control of the herd. And when the monarch of a given territory is harvested by a lucky hunter, there's always another buck ready and willing to move in and take over.

The presumption that the buck tending a large group of does must be a gigantic trophy is often totally false. A smaller, less impressive buck may well have momentarily inherited the harem of his dreams when the real boss went down to a hunter's shot. Eventually he'll be challenged, and the buck able to defend territorial rights will prevail as the new landlord. In the interim, some mayhem may occur until a new true dominant buck is established.

It is the belligerent behavior of herd bucks toward interlopers within their territories during the rut that makes decoying and calling such effective hunting tactics. Always ready for a showdown, a dominant buck is only too ready to attack a stranger in his area. This is especially true when the other buck challenges by standing his ground, seemingly unafraid and snorting his defiance. (See "Decoying & Calling," p. 98.) During the rut, trophy dominant bucks are more vulnerable to hunters than at any other time of the year.

Due to the short, one-time annual estrus period of the pronghorn doe, the rut can be extremely frantic. Breeding season is a taxing time for all adult antelope, especially herd bucks. The short length of the rut is probably in the best interest of the pronghorn's overall well-being because of the high stress inflicted on both bucks and does. It's easy to see how this annual breeding ritual can take its toll on adult antelope, leaving them with a tremendous need to replenish the energy reserves necessary for winter. A longer breeding period of such intensity would easily result in more and prolonged stress and, with winter near, could endanger the overall health of the species.

Hay Bale Buck

Tony Knight, inventor of the Knight in-line percussion muzzleloader, and I were hunting near the small town of Recluse, Wyoming, when we glassed a good 14-inch-class pronghorn buck herding his harem of does into a large irrigated hay field. In less than 30 minutes, the herd passed within 200 hundred yards of a row of huge round hay bales several times. The antelope were being dogged by a second, similarly sized buck, which was apparently intent on stealing away a few of the precious does.

I drove to within 400 yards of the bales, and when the buck with his does worked near the far end of the field, I eased the truck to within a hundred yards of the row and had Tony ease out of the vehicle and slip over to the bales while I slowly drove away. I made my way to a vantage point a half-mile away and watched the show below.

The herd buck fended off the rival buck, chasing him repeatedly back across the field and away from his girlfriends. Nearly 30 minutes later, the buck pushed his small bunch of does nearer and nearer the row of bales where Tony waited. As they passed within 150 yards of the last bale, I watched as a puff of white smoke rolled out from nowhere, followed by the dull boom of Tony's magnum charge of Pyrodex Pellets. At the same instant, the big buck dropped in his tracks.

In a flash, the does ran to the opposite side of the field. As the herd buck lay kicking his last, the rival buck ran down and herded them back into the sage-covered hills. A new dynasty had been established.

- Toby Bridges

Hunting Equipment

Rifles & Scopes

Pronghorn hunting is a rifleman's game. Fleet of foot and sharp-eyed, the pronghorn of the American West has an uncanny ability to keep great distances between it and anything it quickly identifies as dangerous. Where the average shots at whitetails across the country may be well under 100 yards, you can bet that the average shots at pronghorns are much longer. In fact, 200- to 300-yard shots are far more common than shots at less than 100. The ideal pronghorn rifle is a special-purpose, flat-shooting centerfire capable of pinpoint shot placement at extended ranges.

Most Eastern and Midwestern hunters headed west for some antelope hunting generally carry the same rifles they pack back home for their annual deer hunts. While some of these old favorites may be able to stack bullets one right on top of the other at 100 yards, usually the hunter finds that Ol' Betsy lobs the bullet a bit too much to provide the degree of accuracy required for long shots on the prairie.

With a live weight of about 100 pounds, antelope are relatively easy to put down cleanly. However, it is extremely tough to judge the distance to these small animals, especially past 200 yards. A caliber that continues to shoot exceptionally flat between 200 and 300 yards compensates better for misjudging distance than a caliber or bullet selection with a pronounced rainbow trajectory.

In the following section of this book, we will discuss the calibers and ballistics that have become favorites among serious pronghorn hunters. In this chapter, we will look at the types of rifles and scopes that produce the best long-range accuracy.

RIFLE ACTION

Of all the different centerfire rifle types, the bolt-action consistently produces the highest degree of accuracy. Beginning with the earliest bolt-action designs of Paul Mauser in the late 1860s and early 1870s, rifles built on this type of action have been noted for their superior strength and the rigid lock-up of the bolt behind a chambered cartridge. It is this latter trait that contributes so much to the accuracy of a quality bolt-action centerfire rifle.

Quite a few of the newer semi-auto hunting rifles, like the Browning BAR, are winning over a few converts from the bolt-action crowd, especially when quick follow-up shots are needed. However, pronghorn hunting is more often than not a single-shot affair, with very precise placement of the first shot generally determining the success of the stalk or entire hunt. Quality bolt-action rifles like the ever-popular Winchester Model 70, the Remington Model 700, or the Savage Model 110 series tend to deliver accuracy better than any semi-auto, pump or lever-action rifle. This is especially true when the rifle features a good trigger requiring only about 3 pounds of pull.

Single-shot varmint or target rifles in calibers large enough to warrant use on big game continue to gain popularity with the trophy pronghorn hunter. While these rifles often feature very heavy barrels, which can make them quite a load to pack around all day, the guns have been designed and built for long-range shooting. Most also feature premium triggers with a crisp, clean trigger pull. The majority of these guns continue to be built on a bolt-action design, such as the Savage Model 112BT or 112BVSS-S. However some deadly accurate dropping block single shots such as the Ruger No. 1 are also fully capable of shooting tighter groups at 200 yards than the majority of lightweight bolt-action repeaters can punch out at 100 yards.

SCOPES

The finest rifle and quality ammunition are only as effective as the sighting system installed. A top-quality telescopic sight should never be considered a luxury, but rather an investment in downrange performance. Rifle accuracy at longer ranges is virtually impossible without a good scope.

Variable 3- to 9-power scopes represent the best selling models today. This is especially true when mounted on a rifle that sees a variety of uses, from hunting heavy cover for whitetails to shooting at pronghorns on the prairie. Turned down to 3 power, deer at 30 to 40 yards are still easy to find through the scope, while the same sight turned to its highest setting allows the hunter to better refine his hold on an antelope buck out at 200 yards or farther. Many of the heavy barreled, long-range varmint/target rifles rigged specifically for pronghorn shooting are often topped with a variable scope adjustable from 6 to 18 or 24 power. Chambered for some of the hotter calibers, these rifles can be deadly on antelope out to 500 yards.

When selecting a scope for any pronghorn rifle, pay special attention to the scope's eye relief. In other words, make sure there's plenty of distance between your shooting eye and the rear lens of the scope. Here's why: On the prairie you won't always find a handy rock or tree to provide a solid rifle rest. As a result, you'll be forced into shooting from the prone position. When the trigger is pulled from this position, the recoil of the shot comes back against you, and the rifle's muzzle tends to jump more than if you shot from a standing, leaning or sitting position. (In the latter positions, your body rocks slightly rearward to absorb some of the recoil.) It's also fairly common for prone-position shooters to inch up too close to the rear of the scope before firing. So, if your scope has too little eye relief, there's a good chance you'll go home with a different kind of trophy from your hunt – a slight cut above your eye caused by the scope.

As a rule, choose a scope with close to 4 inches of eye relief, and double-check to make sure you're not too close to the rear lens before squeezing off the shot. Forgetting this rule can be painful and could end your hunt.

On big-game hunting rifles, most of today's shooters prefer the crosshair-type reticle. The most popular reticle tends to be what is often referred to as the

"plex" or "duplex" arrangement that features heavy crosshairs at the outer ends, and fine lines where they intersect. By being able to clearly see the point of aim, the shooter can make a precise shot. Since pronghorns are not large animals, exceptionally thick crosshairs or reticles such as the "post" or "dot" will cover most of the chest cavity at long range.

Today there are a number of scopes featuring built-in bullet drop compensators, which eliminate the need to figure how far to hold over a distant target. A hunter simply turns a dial to a setting for a known distance, then holds "dead on" to shoot.

A quality, accurate rifle and a top-notch telescopic sight deserve to be mated with a set of scope bases and rings of the same quality. There isn't much sense in investing $1,000 or more in a new flat-shooting pronghorn rifle and crystal-clear scope if you plan to throw them together with a set of cheap, soft aluminum mounts. Choose the very best bases and rings you can afford, and compare how rigidly the different designs mount up. The more solidly that scope is attached to the rifle, the better it maintains alignment from shot to shot.

SHOOTING POSITIONS

The cardinal rule when shooting at antelope is that "any rest is better than no rest at all." All shooters have a preferred shooting position, and most of the favored positions have the body somewhat upright, i.e. sitting, standing, leaning. However, as we discussed earlier in this chapter, the prone position is often the only option on the prairie. And for someone who has not shot much "laying down," the prone position can at first seem extremely awkward.

Ideally, the prone shooter should try to rest his rifle on a rock, bush, dirt bank, stuffed day pack, or, if your rifle has one, a bipod. The prone position, when performed correctly, is extremely stable and results in good shot placement at long range. Of course, practice makes perfect, and before you head out into pronghorn country, you should get in plenty of 100- to 300-yard practice from this position.

The sitting position is another widely used pronghorn-shooting position. Most shooters are probably more comfortable shooting while sitting than laying prone. This position allows the hunter to crawl into position, turn around and ease into the sitting position without standing and presenting the upright human form that seems to scare the daylights out of antelope. In fact, low-level movement often holds the antelopes' attention while the hunter gets situated. For stability in this position, bend your knees upward and rest your elbows slightly on the inside of each knee cap. Right-handed shooters should face

slightly to the right of their target, left-handed shooters slightly to the left.

While not nearly as steady as either the prone or sitting position, the kneeling position may sometimes be the hunter's only choice, especially where tall grasses or knee-high brush create an obstacle that's impossible to shoot over from the other positions. The right-handed shooter should drop his right knee to the ground, with the left knee up. When the rifle comes up, the left elbow sits atop the left knee, offering some degree of steadiness. While not nearly as rock-solid as either the prone or sitting position, the kneeling stance is definitely more steady than shooting from the standing, off-hand position. The hunter who practices from this position can usually make consistent hits on standing pronghorns out to about 150 yards. If the antelope is farther than that, and the kneeling position is your only option, you may want to consider passing on the shot and trying for that goat later rather than spook him with a missed shot. Worse yet, you could make a poor hit and lose the animal altogether.

A Good Trade

The most effective long-range pronghorn rifle I ever owned came to me largely by chance. I had decided to sell a couple of old aluminum canoes I owned. An old friend wanted the canoes, but didn't have the $400 I was asking for them. He did, however, have a beautiful, like-new Ruger No. 1 "medium-sporter" in the .300 Winchester Magnum caliber. I took the gun on trade.

The rifle sat in my gun cabinet for several months before I pulled a big 6x18 Redfield scope off of a varmint rifle and mounted it on the impressive Ruger single-shot. Shooting two boxes of hot handloads with 165-grain spire-point bullets, I was amazed at how well the rifle grouped at 300 yards. Several three-shot groups were well inside of 3-inches. I had found the antelope rifle I'd use in Wyoming that fall.

Opening morning, a 15-inch buck made the mistake of standing a bit too long as I threw sandbags on the hood of my pickup. I sighted in on the pronghorn out at almost 400 yards (according to my split-image rangefinder). The rifle was sighted to hit dead on at 300 yards, so I held right at the top of the buck's back and eased back on the trigger. The antelope went over like a steel silhouette.

My two hunting partners were so impressed with the shot, they immediately began arguing over who would use the rifle next. And by the time we headed home several days later with three good pronghorn bucks, each of them had taken their bucks at ranges exceeding 400 yards. When I mentioned about halfway home that the rifle was for sale, the bidding began. By the time I pulled into my driveway back in Illinois, one of them owned one heck of a pronghorn rifle!

- Toby Bridges

THE PRONE POSITION should be used whenever possible. It allows you to get down out of the wind and hold your rifle or muzzleloader very steady.

Choosing a Rifle Caliber

Before you purchase a new centerfire rifle for hunting a particular big-game species, you must first determine which caliber delivers the appropriate bullet performance to efficiently harvest that animal.

For example, when selecting a cartridge for pronghorns, you need to ask yourself, "Is this caliber fast, does it shoot flat and is it accurate out to 300 yards and beyond?" These are the traits that generally separate a great pronghorn cartridge from a mediocre one.

A really big antelope buck may weigh a whopping 130 pounds on the hoof – and that's soaking wet! Most mature bucks weigh only 100 to 110 pounds, and mature does are generally closer to 80 or 90 pounds. Simply put, it doesn't take a cannon to put a pronghorn down. In fact, even the most suitable rifles in .25 or .30 caliber are often overkill for this rather small big-game animal.

The fact is, most pronghorns are taken with general-purpose rifles, those used for hunting everything from coyotes to whitetails to elk, and which the hunter most likely already has in his gun cabinet. As a rule, the majority of these centerfire rifles work well enough to hunt pronghorns, even if the magnification of the scope or the cartridge for which it is chambered is less than ideal. Many such rifles can be improved by replacing a basic fixed 4-power scope with a more versatile 3- to 9-power model, or by switching to a lighter, faster bullet for flatter trajectory and extended range. Proper long-range bullet placement on the relatively small pronghorn requires above-average performance on both the part of the shooter and his rifle.

FAVORITE PRONGHORN CARTRIDGES

Let's face it: Pronghorns have probably been taken with just about every rifle caliber ever produced. In some western states, the hunter can legally head out with rifles as small as the .222 Remington or the .223 Remington. In most hunting situations, the fast little 55- and 60-grain bullets, which zip out of these high-velocity .22 centerfires at 3,000 to 3,200 f.p.s., are more than adequate for downing an antelope. And calibers such as the old .220 Swift and .22-250 Remington, with velocities exceeding 3,500 f.p.s. with a 55-grain bullet, will definitely drop a 100-pound pronghorn, even at 300 yards, as long as the shot is perfect. However, if bullet impact is less than perfect, especially at longer ranges, the remaining energy of the tiny .223-inch-diameter bullets out past 300 yards may not be sufficient for cleanly putting down a pronghorn. The best advice is to use the .22 centerfires only for varmints, and pack a rifle chambered for a cartridge that can get the job done whether your shot is 100 yards or 300 yards.

In the following paragraphs, we'll look at a wide range of cartridges and bullet weights well-suited to hunting pronghorns. Often a pronghorn rifle has to double as a mule deer rifle on the same hunt, and the calibers we recommend here will deliver the punch needed to bring down a game animal weighing over 300 pounds. These calibers have won favored status because they're fast, they shoot flat, and out of a quality rifle in the hands of a good shooter, they are deadly accurate.

.243 Winchester

Like a number of today's widely used, commercially loaded cartridges, an early version of the .243 Winchester began as a home-brewed, or "wildcat," cartridge. Winchester introduced the cartridge in 1955 for its Model 70 bolt-action and Model 88 lever-action big-game rifles. The goal was to develop a multi-use varmint- to deer-class rifle delivering the flat-shooting, long-range capabilities of the small high-velocity .22 centerfires, and also pack the energy needed to bring down game as large as whitetails or mule deer. After a strong promotional campaign by the company, the .243 Winchester quickly enjoyed a hearty following, which continues to this day. Savage was one of the very first U.S. arms makers, other than Winchester, to chamber rifles in this caliber. But in time even Remington, which had designed its own 6mm cartridge, gave into consumer demand and

began chambering some of its centerfire rifles for the hot little .24 caliber.

Winchester popularized 80-grain bullets for varmint shooting with the .243, and the use of 100-grain bullets for deer-sized big game, which includes the pronghorn. Today, Winchester continues to offer factory loads for each bullet weight. A 24-inch barreled rifle chambered for the .243 Winchester cartridge produces a muzzle velocity of 3,350 f.p.s. with Super-X ammunition loaded with an 80-grain spire point bullet. Winchester Supreme ammo loaded with a 100-grain spire point bullet is good for 3,090 f.p.s. at the muzzle. Sighted dead-on at 150 yards, the heavier 100-grain bullet prints 0.75 inches high at 100 yards, 2.1 inches low at 200 yards, 5.5 inches below point of aim at 250 yards, and 10.3 inches low all the way out at 300 yards.

6mm Remington

This cartridge was first introduced as the .244 Remington in 1955, originally chambered in the Remington Model 722 bolt-action rifle. It was Remington's answer to the .243 Winchester. However, the Remington barrel was rifled with a 1-turn-in-12-inches rate of rifling twist, and wouldn't shoot the 100-grain bullets as accurately as the Winchester Model 70 in .243 caliber with a quicker 1-turn-in-10-inches rate of twist. In 1963, Remington changed the cartridge designation to 6mm Remington, and the newer Model 700 bolt-action rifles in that caliber were rifled with a faster 1-turn-in-9 inches, handling the .243-inch diameter, 100-grain bullets with authority. Although ballistically slightly superior to the .243 Winchester cartridge, the Remington 6mm never achieved the same popularity.

Remington factory loads with a 100-grain spire-point, boat-tail bullet develop a muzzle velocity of 3,100 f.p.s. out of a 24-inch barrel. Sighted on at 150 yards, the round prints 0.5 inches high at 100, 1.7 inches low at 200, 4.7 inches down at 250 and 9 inches below point of aim at 300 yards.

.270 Winchester

This old favorite of deer hunters across the country was first marketed in 1925, originally chambered in the Winchester Model 54 bolt-action rifles. At the time of its introduction, the .270 Winchester offered better long-range game-taking capabilities than any other big-game cartridge available on the American market. The cartridge is based on a necked-down .30/06 case, and with 130- or 150-grain projectiles, it is a superb pronghorn/deer round.

In its Supreme line of centerfire cartridges, Winchester offers both the 130- and 150-grain spire-point bullets. The lighter bullet leaves the muzzle of a 24-inch barrel at 3,150 f.p.s., and sighted to hit on at 150 yards, the bullet impacts less than 1 inch high at 100, 1.9 inches low at 200, 5.1 inches low at 250 and 9.6 inches low at 300 yards. With a muzzle velocity of 2,930 f.p.s., the slightly heavier 150-grain bullet sighted to hit 1 inch high at 100 yards impacts dead on at 150 yards, 2.4 inches low at 200 yards, 6.4 inches low at 250 yards and 12.2 inches low at 300 yards.

.280 Remington

Here is another Remington cartridge that has suffered from an identity crisis. The chambering was first offered in the Remington Model 740 semi-automatic rifles in 1957, then the following year in the Model 725 bolt-action rifle. Again the .280 Remington is based on a necked-down .30/06 case. Perhaps to give it international appeal, in 1979 Remington changed the designation of the cartridge to the 7mm Remington Express, but went back to its .280 Remington designation within a couple of years.

The cartridge is an extremely versatile choice for a wide range of big game. With heavy 165-grain bullets, it makes a fine elk cartridge, but for pronghorn and deer, bullets weighing 140 or 150 grains are ideal.

Remington factory loads with a 140-grain soft-point Core-Lokt bullet generate 3,000 f.p.s. at the muzzle. When sighted to print dead-on at 150 yards, the spire-point bullet hits about 0.5 inches high at 100 yards, 1.9 inches low at 200 yards, 5.1 inches low at 250 yards, and 9.8 inches low at 300 yards.

7mm Remington Magnum

In 1962 Remington introduced its Model 700 bolt-action rifle and its belted 7mm Remington Magnum cartridge. Today, it's one of the top five when it comes to commercial cartridge sales. Correspondingly, rifles in this caliber are also among the top sellers, and every major U.S. bolt-action centerfire manufacturer, and most importers of foreign-made bolt-action rifles, offer one or more 7mm models. Between Remington, Winchester and Federal, there are factory loads available ranging in bullet weight from 140 to 180 grains. The 165-grain and heavier loads are ideal for game up to the size of moose, while the 140- and 150-grain loads are perfectly suited for pronghorn and deer.

The average muzzle velocity for factory-loaded 140-grain bullets in the 7mm Remington Magnum is between 3,100 and 3,200 f.p.s. Sighted to hit dead-on at 150 yards, a 140-grain spire-point bullet hits just 0.5 inches high at 100 yards, 1.6 inches below point of aim at 200 yards, 4.4 inches low at 250 yards, and 8.5 inches low at 300 yards.

.30/06 Springfield

Often touted as the finest all-purpose big-game rifle cartridge ever developed, the revered .30/06 was originally conceived for the U.S. military. The round was officially adopted as the standard U.S. service cartridge in 1906 (hence the /06 in the name) for the famed Model 1903 Springfield bolt-action rifle. The first sporting rifle to be chambered for the .30/06 was the Winchester Model 1895 lever-action, which was first chambered for the /06 cartridge in 1908. The first bolt-action sporter to be chambered for the cartridge was the Remington Model 30 introduced in 1921, followed by the Winchester Model 54 in 1925. Since those early years as a big-game hunting cartridge, the .30/06 has been chambered in more sporting centerfire rifles than any other cartridge. Today, factory-loaded ammo is available with bullets weighing from 125 to 220 grains.

Winchester offers a speedy 125-grain spire-point load that puts the bullet out of the muzzle of a

Cartridges shown actual size

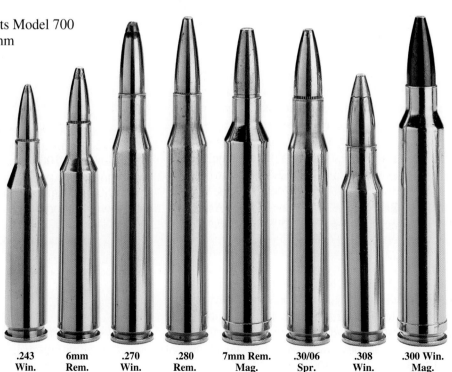

| .243 Win. | 6mm Rem. | .270 Win. | .280 Rem. | 7mm Rem. Mag. | .30/06 Spr. | .308 Win. | .300 Win. Mag. |

CHOOSE a rifle caliber that's comfortable for you to shoot. A young hunter, for example, will shoot much more accurately with a .243 than with a .270 because the smaller caliber has a lot less recoil.

24-inch barrel at 3,140 f.p.s. Zeroed at 150 yards, the light .30 caliber bullet prints not quite 1 inch high at 100 yards, then only 2.1 inches below point of aim at 200 yards. At 250 yards, the bullet impacts the target 5.6 inches low, and 10.7 inches low at 300 yards.

.308 Winchester

The .308 Winchester is not exactly a speed demon when compared to the velocities produced by many of the other cartridges reviewed here, but it's won an excellent reputation for outstanding long-range accuracy. The .308 Winchester, like the .30/06, began life as a military round. The cartridge was originally designated as the 7.62 NATO round, developed along with the predecessor to the old .30/06 M1 Garand, the M14 service rifle. As the .308 Winchester sporting round, it first appeared in the Winchester Model 70 bolt-action and Model 88 lever-action rifles in 1952.

With a Winchester factory-loaded 150-grain spire-point bullet out of a 24-inch barrel, the load produces a muzzle velocity of 2,900 f.p.s. When sighted 1.2 inches high at 100 yards, the round prints dead-on at 150 yards, 2.6 inches low at 200, 7 inches low at 250 and 13.4 inches low at 300 yards.

.300 Winchester Magnum

Introduced in 1963, the .300 Winchester Magnum is basically a .338 Winchester Magnum case necked down to .30 caliber. It has been the most popular of the big .30 caliber magnum cartridges, and more rifles have been chambered for it than any other cartridge in its class. A good selection of factory-loaded ammunition with bullets weighing from 150 to 200 grains makes the cartridge suitable for all North American big game.

A .300 Winchester Mag with a 24-inch barrel sends a 150-grain spire-point bullet out of the muzzle at close to 3,300 f.p.s. However, the best choice for long-range performance on pronghorns is the heavier 180-grain spire-point bullet available in some of the hotter factory loads. These bullets travel around 3,100 f.p.s., maintain high levels of energy, and they're extremely accurate. A 180-grain bullet traveling at this speed and sighted to hit dead-on at 200 yards strikes 1.4 inches high at 100 yards, 1.3 inches high at 150, 2.8 inches low at 250, 6.3 inches low at 300 and 18.3 inches low all the way out at 400.

Handloaded Cartridges

The velocities of just about every cartridge we've looked at here can be improved slightly by handloading your own. By carefully custom-crafting his own ammo, the avid shooter can tweak another 50 to 100 f.p.s. out of most calibers. However, care must always be taken to never exceed the maximum powder charges listed in the loading manuals. There are hundreds of different smokeless powders available, so attempting to handload any cartridge without first consulting a manual is foolish.

Another advantage of handloading your own is being able to load bullet weights not readily available in factory-loaded ammunition, or a bullet of a different shape or configuration. For example, Hornady Manufacturing Company offers 18 different .30-caliber bullets for loading into cartridges like the .30/06 Springfield or .308 Winchester. The most choices offered by an ammunition maker is 9 or 10 different bullets for the .30/06 and only 6 to 8 for the .308 Winchester. Tailoring the bullet and powder charge to a specific rifle generally results in better accuracy, and greater confidence by the hunter.

Wildcat Cartridges

Many of the fine sporting cartridges we now enjoy began through the ingenuity of shooters who were less than happy with the choices available from the gun manufacturers. One such "wildcatter" was Roy Weatherby. He dared to increase case capacities, change the shoulder angles of cartridge cases, have rifles specially chambered for cartridges of his own design, and to develop faster, flatter shooting and harder-hitting loads. His rifles in his calibers, now

available as factory-loaded ammunition, are used around the world by hunters. The .240, .257, .270 and .300 Weatherby Magnums are prized by trophy pronghorn hunters looking for maximum knock-down power at maximum range.

Many rifle-shooting authorities consider the .25/06 Remington the finest wildcat cartridge to ever reach commercial production. Based on a .30/06 Springfield case that's been necked down to .25 caliber, the earliest versions of this cartridge date back to about 1920. However, the round did not develop its full potential until the introduction of modern slow burning powders such as #4350 or #4831. Remington adopted the .25/06 as a standard factory-loaded cartridge in 1969. Shooters find this cartridge extremely well-suited for varmints when handloaded with 75- to 90-grain bullets, and an ideal antelope and deer cartridge with 100- and 120-grain bullets.

Remington .25/06 factory loads are available with both 100- and 120-grain spire-point bullets. The 100-grain projectile leaves the muzzle of a 24-inch rifle barrel at 3,230 f.p.s., and sighted to hit dead-on at 150 yards, the bullet impacts 0.5 inches high at 100 yards, 1.7 inches low at 200, 4.8 inches low at 250 and 9.1 inches below point of aim at 300 yards. The slightly heavier 120-grain bullet is good for 2,990 f.p.s. at the gun's muzzle, and with the same 150-yard zero, the .25/06 rifle is 1.9 inches low at 200, 5.2 inches low at 250, and 10.1 inches low at 300 yards.

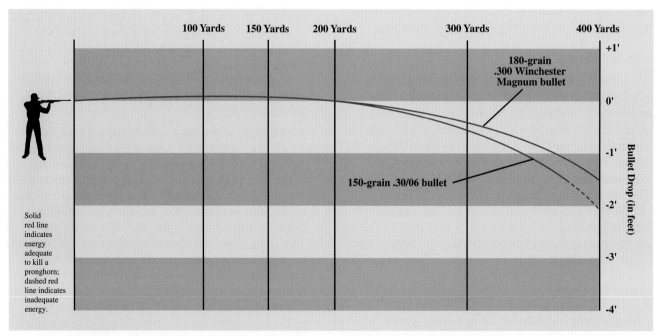

TRAJECTORY AND ENERGY are affected by the choice of rifle caliber and bullet. This chart compares a 180-grain .300 Winchester Magnum bullet and a 150-grain .30/06 bullet. The 180-grain .300 magnum has a flatter trajectory and retains energy longer than the 150-grain .30/06.

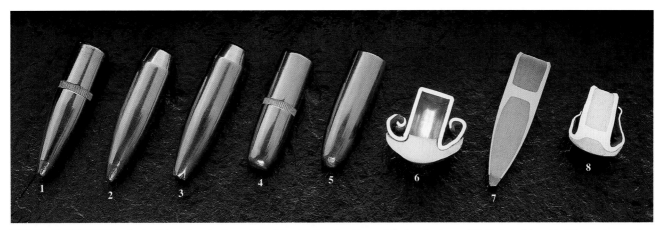

BULLET STYLES include (1) *pointed*, streamlined for high velocity and flat trajectory. (2) *Pointed boat tail* has a tapered base to reduce drag even more. (3) *Hollow* points mushroom rapidly. (4) *Flat* and (5) *round* points are often used in rifles with tubular magazines. Their blunt points will not detonate cartridges ahead of them, but result in relatively slow flight and short range. (6) Mushroomed bullet shows expansion. (7) *Nosler™ partition* (cross-section) has a thin-walled front core and thick-walled rear core. (8) Mushroomed Nosler shows expansion in front, but the rear core keeps its shape.

Most wildcat cartridge designers fail to ever be as widely recognized as Weatherby for their efforts. One such shooter is Henry Ball of Greensboro, North Carolina. In his local area, and among a small group of "in" long-range benchrest shooters, he's known for his super-accurate, high-velocity wildcat calibers. For instance, take his 7mm H&B Magnum, which gets a 140-grain spire-point bullet out of the muzzle at an earth-shattering 3,680 f.p.s. Zeroed dead-on at 200 yards, this flat-shooting 7mm wildcat prints less than 1 inch high at 100 yards and less than 2 inches low at 300 yards. At 400 yards the 140-grain bullet hits only about 8 inches low and, for the record, is still travelling along at 2,760 f.p.s.

Ball's .257 B&B Magnum takes a 100-grain spire-point to 4,022 f.p.s. at the muzzle, and if the shooter sights in dead-on at 400 yards, the bullet would impact just 2.9 inches high at 100 yards, 4.9 inches high at 200 yards, and 4.2 inches high at 300 yards. In other words, the pronghorn hunter could hold dead center all the way out to 450 yards, where the bullet impacts just 3.5 inches low, and still put the speedy 100-grain bullet squarely through the animal's chest cavity.

Oldies But Goodies

Through the years, a number of good pronghorn cartridges have come and gone, replaced by hotter, better-performing case designs. Some of these obsolete cartridges were simply victims of falling too closely in between other cartridges that tended to do a better job. These include the .250/3000 (or .250 Savage), .257 Roberts, .264 Winchester Magnum and the old .284 Winchester. Except for an occasional limited run in these calibers, most of today's rifle makers don't chamber for these cartridges any longer.

However, with a 100- to 130-grain bullet, these cartridges can effectively take pronghorns out to 300 yards, and farther yet with the .264 Winchester Magnum. Factory-loaded ammo is still offered for all of these oldies, but the serious pronghorn hunter may find that the best performance is from hand-loads.

TRAJECTORY

Perhaps the most important attribute of a good open-country cartridge is a flat trajectory. It is the first requirement of a suitable antelope round. Simply speaking, the less a bullet rises or drops below the point of aim, the better it is for long-range shooting. The flight of the bullet is known as trajectory and is generally expressed in tables as inches above or below line-of-sight at different distances. A cartridge that is said to have a flat trajectory displays noticeably less drop at longer ranges compared to cartridges with a more pronounced rainbow bullet path.

Under certain conditions and in some terrain, the pronghorn hunter may find that he can easily crawl or sneak within 100 yards of unsuspecting antelope, setting up an easy shot for just about any centerfire rifle, even the old .30/30 Winchester, which really lobs bullets at distances over 150 yards. But don't always count on superior stalking skills to get you within range – not with these sharp, wary game animals. Good, long-range shooting has downed more pronghorns than stealth. The rifle, cartridge and bullet weight you choose should allow you to take a shot all the way out to 300 yards, which means a rifle must put a 100- to 150-grain bullet out of the muzzle at 3,000 or more feet per second. The pronghorn rifle sighted to hit dead-on at 200 yards should put the bullet no more than 2 to 3 inches high at 100

My Favorite Goat Cartridge

Back in 1958, Winchester introduced a new high-velocity centerfire cartridge, the .264 Winchester Magnum, which was based on the belted .458 Winchester Magnum case necked-down to 6.5mm (.264-inch). The company immediately began promoting its new offering as the answer to the North American big-game hunter's dream. Here was a single cartridge that could be used to take most big-game species on the continent.

Factory loads for this cartridge are usually matched with 100- or 140-grain bullets. The hunter willing to hand-load, however, has several dozen different bullet designs available, each varying in weight (85 to 160 grains), construction and tip type. The many combinations make this an extremely versatile cartridge. Bullets of 100 to 120 grains are ideal for pronghorns, the 140-grain bullets are adequate for deer, mountain sheep and goats, and the hefty, slightly round-nosed 160-grain bullets are more than adequate for elk, caribou and even moose.

It was the touted versatility of the .264 Winchester Magnum that attracted me to it more than 30 years ago when I was shopping for my first big-game rifle. And wouldn't you know it, as soon as I owned one and fell in love with it, the cartridge began to receive a bad rap for excessive erosion of the barrel's rifling just ahead of the chamber, supposedly caused by the hot-burning powder charges and super-sonic velocities. Due to these rumors, the .264 met an early demise.

After more than 30 years of owning and shooting my .264 rifle, I'm happy to report that it still shoots great. Extensive tests by several powder companies have now established that the fears that the barrel would be easily and quickly be "shot out" were unfounded. A number of .264 rifles have surpassed 3,000 hot-loaded rounds without any noticeable effect on the rifling.

My .264 was and still is my favorite antelope gun. My 140-grain handloads perform admirably in the gun, and although muzzle velocities exceed 3,000 f.p.s., the barrel on my old Remington Model 700 has not succumbed to excessive wear. It will still routinely shoot a 1-inch group at 100 yards. On occasion, when I'm having a very good day, the rifle and handloads print under 1 inch.

- Don Oster

---

yards, and no more than 7 to 8 inches low at 300 yards. Trajectory this flat allows the hunter to hold dead-on all the way out to about 250 yards, then only 6 to 8 inches above his normal hold when attempting a 300- to 325-yard shot.

Most big-game hunting experts agree that it takes somewhere around 1,000 foot-pounds of energy to cleanly down a whitetail. While the same amount of energy may not be required to bring down prong-horns, any cartridge that continues to deliver 1,000 foot-pounds of energy at the longer ranges definitely puts one of the prairie goats down on the spot, provided the bullet is placed where it needs to go.

BULLET WEIGHT, SHAPE AND CONSTRUCTION

Today's bullets come in a wide range of shapes, nose types and construction. While the selection gives the knowledgeable shooter better choices for hunting a particular species, or in a particular type of cover, the variety also makes it harder for the less-know-ledgeable hunter to head out with the best bullet design for antelope.

Pronghorn hunting doesn't require a heavily constructed bullet. In fact, pronghorns are relatively thin-skinned, and although muscular for their size, they simply aren't very big. Any quality, expanding bullet weighing between 100 to 150 grains will penetrate sufficiently to do needed damage to the animal's vitals. Good hits are lethal. The importance of the bullet's shape relates to its ability to maintain velocity, a true course and flat trajectory in flight. Subsequently, sharp-tipped spire-point bullets, especially those featuring a tapered boat-tail base, are more aerodynamic than round-nosed flat-tail bullets. The bullet with the sleeker design offers less wind resistance and holds trajectory better.

ACCURACY TESTING - GROUPING

Confidence in a rifle and load only comes from accuracy tests prior to the hunt. An enjoyable part of any pronghorn hunt is fine-tuning the rifle and load to print precisely where you want it at 100, 200 and 300 yards. And before ever attempting a shot at an antelope, the hunter needs to spend plenty of time at the range shooting at these distances. When you can keep all of your hits in the "kill zone" at these distances, you'll have the confidence to make a good shot when the opportunity arises.

Most hunters use factory loads, and can learn a lot about how much the bullet drops at different ranges from ballistics tables published by the ammunition manufacturer. However, there is still no substitute for getting out and shooting – and shooting, and shooting. Just because a rifle is of a particular caliber doesn't mean that it turns in optimum accuracy with just any factory ammunition. It's a well-known fact

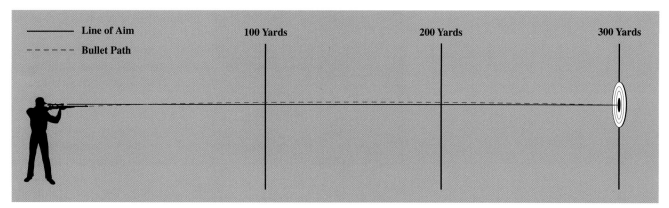

SIGHT IN your rifle so the bullet hits just above the point of aim at 100 yards. For most flat-shooting cartridges, you should zero in 2 to 3 inches high; the exact distance depends on the trajectory of your bullet. By sighting in this way, you can aim dead-on at a pronghorn at any range up to 300 yards. The bullet will hit slightly high or low, depending on the range, but will strike somewhere in the animal's vital area.

that a Remington rifle often shoots best with Winchester ammo, or vice versa. It's imperative that a new rifle be tested with a variety of ammunition brands, and possibly even several different bullet weights to find the ideal combination. As a bonus, the practice you get through testing greatly improves your shooting ability.

It is virtually impossible to properly sight in a rifle and get it to consistently produce tight groups unless it is fired from a bench rest or other solid shooting platform. Always use sandbags or a shooting rest to help eliminate human error. Make adjustments to the scope until the rifle is hitting where you would like it, usually 1 to 2 inches above point of aim at 100 yards for most pronghorn rifles. Next, shoot three shots at 100 yards, giving the barrel 4 or 5 minutes to cool down between each shot. Measure the distance between the centers of the two bullet holes farthest apart. You should expect the group with a suitable cartridge to measure no more than 1½ inches from center to center. If your group measures less than 1 inch, you not only are an excellent shot, but you have found an excellent combination for your rifle. Lift your eyes to the heavens and give thanks.

If your groups repeatedly measure more than 3 inches, try another brand of ammunition or a different bullet weight. Although you most likely won't have a rest as solid as a bench or sandbags when shooting at antelope in the field, you must first prove the ability of your rifle to print a tight group before relying on it under hunting conditions.

TRAJECTORY TEST

Once you have acceptable groups at 100 yards, it's time to do some shooting at 200, 300 and possibly even 400 yards. With the rifle sighted 1 to 2 inches high at 100 yards, it should print dead-on somewhere

between 150 and 200 yards. Look at the trajectories given for the cartridges covered earlier in this section and you'll have a better idea of what to expect. For example, take the .270 Winchester with a 150-grain factory load. Sighted in at 1 inch high at 100 yards, a spire-pointed projectile hits dead-on at 150, about 1.9 inches low at 200, 5.1 inches low at 250 and 9.6 inches low at 300.

You need to know these same points of impact for your rifle and bullet combination. And even if you have trajectory tables for reference, you still need to get out and pop a few rounds at the longer distances to confirm bullet drop at extended ranges. For future reference, record the trajectory of your rifle and load; it could come in handy later. Many shooters tape a trajectory table right to the butt of their stock for quick reference in the field.

The vitals of a pronghorn are found in an area measuring about 10 inches square, overlapping and slightly to the rear of the front shoulder. Range estimation becomes key to making a good shot, especially once the trajectory of your rifle and load begins to drop significantly below point of aim. This is where one of the lightweight laser rangefinders are handy. They totally eliminate the guesswork. Also, the scope on the rifle can dictate to some degree a hunter's maximum effective range. If it does not offer enough magnification, or if it features a heavy reticle, which makes precise shot placement difficult much past 250 yards, then shots beyond that distance are ill-advised, chancy and will likely result in the distasteful event of wounded game.

Muzzleloaders

Depending on the source of the information, there are an estimated 2½ to 3 million muzzleloading hunters in the country today. This is easily five to six times as many frontstuffers headed into the field each fall as there were just 25 years ago. Why the sudden interest in hunting with slow-to-load rifles of old-fashioned design? First, an ever growing whitetail population continues to offer greater and longer hunting opportunities, and game departments where this outstanding big-game animal is found have established new seasons in their attempts to increase harvest and curb continued growth. The special muzzleloading seasons offer additional hunting time, and in many states permit the additional harvest of game. Secondly, the muzzleloading rifles used by the majority of today's hunters are not old-fashioned.

The frontloading rifles popular with shooters during the 1960s and 70s were of very traditional design.

Back then, nostalgia played a major role in why modern-day shooters turned to a firearm from the past. It was simply the challenge of mastering a 100- to 200-year-old firearms design that fascinated the slowly growing number of so-called "black-powder shooters." It was also during this same period that a few states began to establish the special muzzleloading deer seasons, partly to give hunters with an historical mindset their own special season, partly to determine if muzzleloading could play a role in the overall game management plan.

As long as the muzzleloader hunting regulations were traditionally oriented, requiring rifles and projectiles replicating those used before the introduction of breech-loading firearms, the number of muzzleloading hunters in the country remained relatively low. However, as whitetail herds and other big-game herds continued to grow, more and more modern firearm hunters began to invade the ranks of die-hard traditional muzzleloading shooters. And with them they brought changes in the style of frontloading firearm they preferred. During the 1980s, we saw the introduction of the practical in-line percussion ignition muzzleloader, and the growing popularity of still more advanced designs that have taken over the muzzleloading industry since. Today, these extremely modern muzzleloading big-game rifles represent close to 75 percent of all muzzleloader sales. The success enjoyed while hunting the whitetail with a muzzleloader has encouraged an ever-growing number of hunters to use their guns for hunting a wide range of other big game, including pronghorns.

Muzzleloading has matured into a performance-driven hunting sport, and the tack-driving scope-sighted frontloading rifles preferred by the majority of today's hunters are a far cry from the old-fashioned rifles carried West by the likes of Lewis and Clark, Jim Bridger or Kit Carson. In fact, when time is taken to carefully match the proper plastic sabot and jacketed handgun bullet for a modern in-line ignition rifle, the gun is fully capable of printing tighter 100-yard groups than many out-of-the-box centerfire rifles.

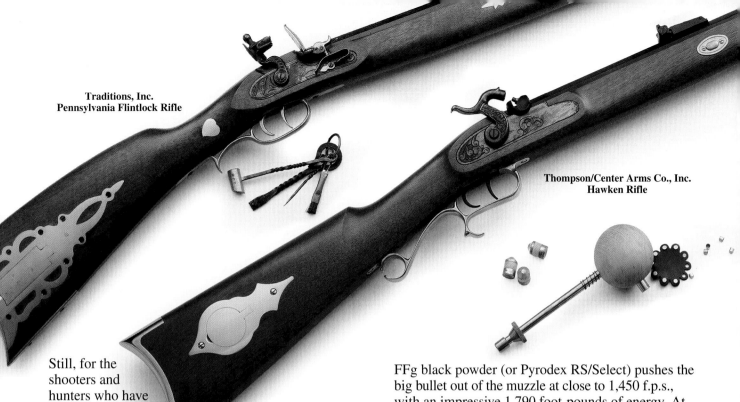

Traditions, Inc.
Pennsylvania Flintlock Rifle

Thompson/Center Arms Co., Inc.
Hawken Rifle

Still, for the shooters and hunters who have turned to muzzleloading for a portal through which they can step back in time, there remains a great selection of authentically styled reproductions. The trustworthy Thompson/Center Arms Hawken rifle, available in .50 or .54 caliber, remains one of the more popular traditional "side-hammer" frontloaders. The 1-turn-in-48-inches rate of rifling twist found in the 28-inch octagon barrel permits the use of either a patched round ball or heavy "maxi" style conical bullet. With 90 to 100 grains (measured by volume) of FFg black powder or Pyrodex RS/Select, a rifle loaded with a soft lead ball will effectively take big game out to around 100 yards, and a gun loaded with one of the heavier lead conical bullets is effective to about 150 yards.

The .50 caliber Thompson/Center Arms Hawken loaded with a cotton-cloth-patched, 180-grain, .490-inch-diameter pure lead round ball and 90 grains of FFg black powder develops a muzzle velocity of around 1,750 f.p.s. This translates into 1,230 foot-pounds of energy at the muzzle. However, being a perfect sphere, the ball looses velocity quickly, along with needed game-taking energy. By the time this load reaches 100 yards, the ball is moving along at only about 970 f.p.s., hitting with only 378 foot-pounds of energy. A perfect hit on a pronghorn would bring it down, but the hunter should never push the ineffectiveness of a round ball beyond 100 yards.

Being so much heavier, a 385-grain Buffalo Bullet or Hornady Great Plains Bullet for a .50 caliber Hawken requires a little more powder to get it rolling along at acceptable velocity. An even 100-grain charge of

FFg black powder (or Pyrodex RS/Select) pushes the big bullet out of the muzzle at close to 1,450 f.p.s., with an impressive 1,790 foot-pounds of energy. At 100 yards, the big bullet still drives home with close to 1,300 foot-pounds of energy, or about three times the energy the lighter round ball has remaining at the same distance. At 150 yards, the heavy conical is still good for more than 1,100 foot-pounds of energy, but really begins to drop. Sighted dead-on at 100 yards, the bullet would print more than 8 inches low at 150.

The modern in-line ignition rifles immediately appealed to the new breed of muzzleloading hunter for several reasons. Not only are the guns lighter and better handling, with modern rifle-type stocks and other features, these frontloaders deliver more sure-fire ignition and tend to turn in superior game-taking performance with a wide range of modern saboted bullets. This style of rifle was initially popularized by the Knight MK-85, designed by rural Missouri gunsmith William "Tony" Knight and introduced in 1985. The basic plunger-hammer design of this inline has been copied by most other muzzleloading gun manufacturers, and today we have a great selection of these and improved "bolt-action" in-line ignition muzzleloaders from which to choose.

With only a few exceptions, most of these in-lines feature rifling that spins with a fast 1-turn-in-24- to 32-inches rate of twist. While the barrels will turn in very impressive downrange groups with big heavy conical "maxi" style bullets, these rifles have been designed and built to be shot with modern plastic sabots and any of a wide range of jacketed or all-copper bullets.

The beauty of the sabot projectile system is that it allows the muzzleloading hunter to better match the bullet to the game being hunted. For instance, out of the same .50-caliber in-line muzzleloader, the hunter can load and shoot bullet weights from as light as 175 grains to as hefty as 325 grains, allowing him to tailor a load specifically for everything from varmints to moose. While some of today's advanced in-line rifles may tend to turn in their best performance with a longer, heavier bullet, others show a real preference for a considerably shorter, lighter bullet. However, all tend to shoot very well with a saboted bullet weighing 240 to 260 grains, which is ideal for hunting pronghorns.

With a 100-grain charge of Pyrodex Select, a Remington Model 700ML or Ruger Model 77/50, both with 24-inch .50 caliber barrels and 1-turn-in-28-inches rifling twist, pushes a saboted .452-inch diameter 250-grain Hornady jacketed XTP hollow-point out of the muzzle at around 1,640 f.p.s. This load generates 1,500 foot-pounds of energy. At 100 yards, it's still good for around 1,050 foot-pounds of knockdown power, and retains about 850 foot-pounds of energy

240-grain jacketed Hornady bullet with plastic sabot

all the way out to 150 yards. After that, it really begins to lose steam. Sighted dead-on at 100 yards, the load would print just shy of 2 inches high at 50 and 6.3 inches low at 150 yards.

The Knight D.I.S.C. Rifle and Thompson/Center Arms Encore 209x50 Magnum rifles vary greatly in design, but are similar in performance. The Knight rifle is a unique bolt-action design utilizing a tiny plastic disc and No. 209 primer for ignition, while the Encore 209x50 Magnum is a break-open action muzzleloader, but it too relies on a hot shotshell primer for ignition. The manufacturers of these rifles have heavily promoted the use of three 50-grain Pyrodex Pellets, for a total powder charge of 150 grains. And when such "magnum" powder charges are loaded behind a saboted 250-grain bullet like the Hornady XTP, muzzle velocities are in the 2,000 f.p.s. range, generating energy levels exceeding 2,200 foot-pounds. Likewise, these hotter loads produce a considerably flatter trajectory. Sighted dead-on at 100 yards, either of these rifles with a 26-inch barrel hits only 3 inches low at 150, and close to 14 inches low at 200 yards, where the bullet will still be moving along with more than 1,200 foot-pounds of energy.

As hot as these two very modern in-line ignition rifles may seem, there is now a new leader when it comes to high-performance hunting muzzleloaders, the Savage Model 10ML. What sets this .50-caliber, bolt-action, in-line ignition muzzleloader apart from any other muzzleloader ever manufactured is that for the first time, we now have a frontloading rifle engineered to be loaded and shot with modern smokeless powders. While the Model 10ML performs as well as any other in-line rifle with loads of Pyrodex or Pyrodex Pellets, this muzzleloader really shows its stuff when loaded with powders like IMR-4227, Accurate Arms XMP-5744 or Vihtavouri N110.

With a 45-grain charge (measured by weight, not by volume) of Accurate Arms XMP-5744 behind a 250-grain Hornady .45 XTP loaded with a Muzzleload Magnum Products high-pressure sabot, this rifle produces a muzzle velocity of about 2,275 f.p.s., with more than 2,800 foot-pounds of energy. Sighted to print dead-on at 100 yards, the load prints less than 2 inches low at 150, and about 9 inches low at 200 yards. At the longer range, this load is still good for more than 1,600 foot-pounds of energy. As the 250-grain bullet passes the 250-yard mark, it still hits with more than 1,000 foot-pounds of remaining energy, but bullet drop is close to 20 inches.

EFFECTIVE RANGE. For pronghorn, the maximum effective range of the traditionally styled muzzleloader with a patched round ball is under 100 yards. An accurate side-hammer rifle shooting a

Savage Model 10ML in-line muzzleloader

heavy conical bullet with 100 to 110 grains of FFg black powder or Pyrodex "RS/Select" has enough energy to down a pronghorn at slightly past 150 yards, provided the shooter knows the exact drop and how to allow for it once the bullet gets much past 125 yards.

Just about any of the modern in-line ignition rifles loaded with 100 grains of Pyrodex, either loose-grain RS/Select or two of the 50-grain Pyrodex Pellets, and a saboted 240- to 260-grain jacketed handgun bullet or all-copper bullet like the Barnes Expander-MZ, should deliver the punch and accuracy to down pronghorns out to about 175 yards. The hotter primer-ignited in-lines like the Knight D.I.S.C. rifle and Thompson/Center Arms Encore 209x50 Magnum with heavy 150-grain Pyrodex Pellet loads can extend effective range out to slightly past 200 yards. And the new Savage Model 10ML still delivers pronghorn-stopping energy levels out to beyond

250 yards, provided the shooter can learn to contend with the excessive drop of the bullet past 200 yards.

Muzzleloading has become more performance-driven than at any time in the past. Muzzleloader hunters include those who are more shooter than hunter, as well as those who are more hunter than shooter. The shooter may take pride in making that long-range shot on a good buck, while the hunter may pride himself in his ability to slip in close for a cinch shot with a patched round ball loaded in a traditional percussion or flintlock rifle. If a muzzleloader pronghorn hunt is in your future, just be sure that you know the effective range of your rifle and load, and the limits of your own shooting ability.

NOTE: Never load modern smokeless powders in any muzzleloader other than the Savage Model 10ML. No other muzzleloader has been built to withstand the high pressures of these powders.

Patience Pays Off

Pronghorns have a way of wearing on the muzzleloading hunter's patience. Standing out on an open rise, visible for miles, antelope will sucker you into attempting a stalk time after time. However, as good as your approach may have been, once you get to within 250 yards, more often than not you'll discover that you've gotten as close as the terrain or cover permits. And that darn pronghorn buck seems to always be just 100 or so yards outside of the effective range of your frontloader.

Outdoor writer Tom Fegely and I were having one of those days in north central Wyoming a few years back. He and I had spent 4 days chasing mule deer in a remote wilderness tract of Bureau of Land Management range, then shifted out onto the open plains for a crack at antelope. Tom had a full day to fill his pronghorn tag before having to climb back on an airplane and fly home to Pennsylvania. Since I had several more days to hunt, we decided to concentrate on getting Tom's tag filled.

A half-dozen times that morning we glassed good bucks from the pickup, and I would drop Tom off at a point where he could take advantage of the terrain and make a stalk. Each

Tom Fegely and his trophy pronghorn

time, he would come up about 150 yards shy of the effective range of his scoped .50-caliber Knight MK-85.

The sun was beginning to slowly sink into the horizon when we spotted a good buck with a half-dozen does out in a hay field. We were able to approach within 300 yards of the antelope, thanks to a couple of old ranch buildings. I had Tom stay where he was, then returned to the pickup and eased back away from the hay field. Fifteen minutes later, I slowly rolled up to the fence line on the other side of the field, about 300 yards from the antelope. Nervously, they watched the shiny, bright red truck. Then they began working toward the other side of the field . . . and the waiting hunter. Nearly 40 minutes later, those pronghorns were standing just 125 yards from the old shed where Tom watched through his scope. The big buck never knew what hit him as the saboted 260-grain Speer .45-caliber jacketed-hollow point found its mark.

Patience and persistence can be as valuable to the muzzleloading hunter as a deadly accurate rifle and load.

- Toby Bridges

Bowhunting the West

The serious centerfire rifle hunter may own a rack full of guns, with a rifle specifically matched with a particular scope and bullet weight for hunting a specific species of game, such as the pronghorn. However, not many successful bowhunters use one bow for deer, another for elk, then put together a matched rig just for antelope.

In fact, the truly serious bowhunter uses just one bow for everything. And while he or she may have a similar or identical back-up bow, you can bet that most will use the very same bow, arrows and even broadheads for hunting whatever big game they're after. Why? Because the overall feel of the bow at full draw, which comes from many hours of dedicated practice with a particular setup, creates a familiarity with your equipment that is so vital to precise shot placement.

In the not-so-distant past, any hunter venturing out after pronghorns with sticks and feathers in hand would have earned an award for extreme optimism and courage. The odds of success were so stacked against the hunter that only a very few of the most skilled bowhunters even tried. But today, with the modern developments in bowhunting equipment, plus new hunting techniques such as decoying, all of that has changed.

In fact, pronghorns have become increasingly popular with bowhunters. Across much of the West, special archery antelope seasons are found in many areas, giving bowhunters first crack at this wary game animal. However, even though the pronghorns may not have yet been pushed around by rifle hunters, they're still no pushovers.

While bowhunting for any big-game animal presents a formidable challenge, getting within bow-and-arrow range of such a quick-sighted and fleet-footed animal as the pronghorn is additionally challenging. Combine the honed senses of antelope with the normally wide-open habitat where they're found, and the likelihood of getting one shooting opportunity may at first seem out of the realm of possibility. Fortunately, newly developed hunting techniques, combined with extreme hunter patience, can and will bring antelope to the bowhunter. Often the rewards are a fine buck, one that qualifies for the coveted Pope and Young Club record book.

Today's modern compound bows are nothing short of a marvel in engineering ingenuity. Matched with the proper arrow and broadhead, they shoot faster and flatter than any bow available in the past. Since the earliest Allen compound bows of the late 1960s, manufacturers have continuously improved the design of the concept, incorporating modern space-age materials to produce bows today with arrow speeds well over 300 fps. This is about twice the speed available from many of the recurve-style bows used in the 1950s and 60s.

In the hands of an extremely skilled archer, the modern compound bow is lethal on big game out to about 50 yards. However, most bowhunters have a maximum range of about 30 yards, and even at this distance consistency only comes from many hours of practice. Some archery pronghorn hunters like to boast about making 50-yard-plus shots, but once the distance is over 30 yards, shots become increasingly risky, and the likelihood of wounding a pronghorn increases significantly.

Long-range shots should be avoided because of three factors: wind, animal movement/position, and distance estimation. The first factor, wind, should be self-explanatory. Howling winds are a constant companion in pronghorn country, and arrows are easily blown off course by the 20 to 30 mph breezes common on a "calm" day.

The second factor, animal movement/position, is the one most hunters fail to consider before taking a long shot. All a pronghorn has to do is begin walking, turn suddenly, or run at the moment you release the arrow and you're going to have a bad hit. If you're lucky, you'll miss the animal completely.

The third factor, distance estimation, typically affects hunters who normally hunt in forested habitats. These hunters usually learn to use trees as reference points for judging distance, and the prairie lacks trees. Most of these hunters estimate that an antelope is much closer than it actually is, and this spells trouble when choosing the correct sight pin on their bow.

Perhaps the best archery practice is to bring a 3-D target with you on your western hunt. This way, you can learn first-hand how hard the wind blows, and how difficult it is to accurately judge distance on the prairie.

Clothing & Footwear

Antelope hunting doesn't require any special clothing, other than those garments needed to keep you comfortable and legal (for example, fluorescent orange during the gun season). However, if there's one bit of advice a veteran hunter would pass on to someone looking at their first try at pronghorns, it would be to go prepared for extreme weather changes. Temperatures on the northern prairies during the September and October antelope seasons can range from hot, sweaty shirtsleeve weather to bone-chilling cold, often on the very same day.

During most years, fall is a pleasant time to be outdoors in the central western states. Generally speaking, the pronghorn hunter can usually get by wearing a pair of jeans, a medium-weight flannel or chamois shirt and a lightweight jacket. However, when headed west, always keep in mind that winter can arrive quickly. Many mornings that begin in the 50s can see heavy snow and temperatures in the 20s or 30s by evening. A day or two later, temperatures may shoot into the 90s.

While pronghorns are most commonly found in arid to semi-arid regions, where annual rainfall is usually less than 15 inches, the scattered fall rains frequently moving into the central plains can be cold and hard. And when temperatures continue to drop, the precipitation changes to snow. So be sure to throw in some quality lightweight rain wear, plus at least one set of insulated outerwear.

Most of the time you could probably hunt in sneakers, but a good pair of leather boots does a much better job of protecting your toes and feet from the intrusion of cactus spikes. Many pronghorn hunters think that the ultimate footwear is a lightweight, fully waterproof, leather hiking boot. Remember, you're hunting on the prairie and not in the mountains, so don't get a hiking boot with a deep tread pattern. If you get rain, the prairie mud will clog the deep treads and make each boot heavy and difficult to walk in. You're far better off with a shallow- to medium-tread hiking boot.

Of course, comfortable footwear is a must. Even if you spend a lot of time glassing from the pickup, chances are you'll still have to do quite a bit of walking, and crawling. Antelope don't always stand near two-track roads waiting for you to show up, and chances are you'll see more animals by hiking away from the easy-access areas.

Normally, you'll spot a herd in the distance, then hike to some vantage point to better size up a buck's horns. In this open country, what looks like a little walk to the top of the next hill can turn out to be a mile hike. And if the buck is a shooter, you may spend the rest of the morning or afternoon, on foot, trying to get closer for a shot. Do this several times a day and, before you know it, you've walked many miles. Your feet will appreciate a pair of comfortable boots.

No antelope hunt is complete without some crawling. And often you'll need to do a lot of crawling to keep out of sight and inch your way to within shooting range. No matter where you spot a herd, it always seems that in your final approach, there's a mile or more of open

HIKING BOOTS are ideal for pronghorn hunting. The best models, like these Irish Setter Scouts, are comfortable, lightweight, tough and waterproof. In hot weather, wear a pair of Coolmax® socks, which are designed to keep your feet both cool and dry.

terrain between the last good cover and the place where the animals are cautiously watching for any sign of trouble. It just wouldn't be antelope hunting unless you crawled great distances. And along the way you're sure to encounter a zillion sharp little rocks. However, the rocks are only a minor part of the prone antelope hunter's worries.

It seems that in spite of your best efforts to avoid them, the spikes from cactuses will somehow get you. Cactuses will poke their spikes into your knees and elbows, then go on to invade places you'll swear are impossible. And for several months after the season ends, you'll still be pulling the needlelike buggers out as deeply imbedded spines slowly work their way back to the skin's surface. Savvy antelope hunters avoid cactus spines in the most obvious places by wearing padded leather knee and elbow pads, and often a full set of leather leg chaps. Such protection saves you some of the pain, aggravation and tediousness of pulling out the tiny spines. It's also advisable to wear a pair of thick leather gloves.

Bowhunters have a great selection of camouflaged clothing from which to choose. Some of the darker woods-type patterns, which are very popular in the hardwoods of the Midwest and East, are ideal for hunting in sagebrush-covered terrain. However, when hunting really open country covered primarily by tan and almost yellow-colored grasses, these dark patterns appear as a dark blob when seen from a distance. Several of the lighter-colored patterns, often developed for use in marshy areas by waterfowlers, actually do a better job of breaking up your silhouette and blending you into the surroundings.

With or without camouflage, the bowhunter often has his work cut out for him. Getting to within bow range of a pronghorn takes some doing. Most successful bowhunters rely on the use of a decoy and calling, or wait patiently in a blind near a waterhole, fence crossing or trail. Even then, the movement of getting the bow to full draw spooks many antelope. For this reason, many bowhunters "on stand" use a modern portable blind for concealment.

Few pronghorn hunters pay a great amount of attention to scent-reducing clothing, scent-eliminating sprays or cover scents. This is especially true among rifle hunters, who have the advantage of a long distance between them and their quarry. However, try sneaking toward a herd with the wind at your back and all you'll likely see of them are their white rumps bouncing

over the horizon. Bow and muzzleloading hunters in pursuit of pronghorn are well advised to take the same scent-control precautions as whitetail hunters. And whenever possible, approach the animals with the wind in your face.

Expect the Unexpected

A few years ago, I spotted a huge 16-inch buck. I crawled for nearly a half mile in an attempt to get within rifle range, only to watch the buck and seven does cross over a ridge and out of sight. About 30 minutes later, I eased to the top of the ridge and spotted the herd leisurely standing in the valley below. I knew that if I could slip into a nearby draw without being spotted, the deep wash below would allow me to easily get within range.

I put my plan into action and, as I slipped down the backside of the ridge, I looked back at my truck parked nearly 2 miles away. I also noticed that it was snowing lightly where the truck sat, and that the falling flakes were slowly moving in my direction. By the time I crawled across the ridge top to drop into the narrow draw, snow was lightly falling around me and I could no longer see the truck.

Everything was going perfectly. Before closing the last 500 yards on the antelope, I eased to the top of the wash and spotted them, some standing and some bedded, right where I had last seen them. But the snow was falling harder, making it more difficult to see. By the time I got to within 200 yards from the antelope, I could barely see 75 yards. Then, it really began to snow hard, and with the falling snow came falling temperatures.

I waited 30 minutes and the storm didn't let up. The ground was soon covered with 4 inches of the white stuff, and I decided I'd better find my way back to the truck. I certainly wasn't dressed for this type of weather, and although I badly wanted the huge buck, no animal was worth dying for.

As I started back, I realized that I wasn't sure of my directions. I no longer had definite landmarks to tell me if I was still headed towards my truck. Then, the wind began to howl. My light jacket wasn't enough, and I was soon chilled to the bone.

After a lot of walking, I figured I had to be close to my pickup. But with just 50 yards of visibility, it was like searching for a needle in a haystack. I finally settled in behind a couple of big boulders and waited. Out of the 40 mph winds, the temperature was tolerable. Two hours later, the storm let up, and I spotted my truck just a few hundred yards away. That day I learned to pack for any weather. Not doing so cost me a shot at one of the biggest bucks I've ever seen.

- Toby Bridges

73

Hunting Accessories

When outfitting yourself for almost any type of big-game hunting, you'll discover a few so-called "accessories" that contribute so greatly to the success of the hunt they actually become "necessities." Pronghorn hunting is no exception, and may require a number of items seldom used in the white-tail woods. Here is a look at a variety of gear that can make any antelope hunt more enjoyable, more comfortable and most important of all, more successful. You may already own many of these items, while some of the others are sure to end up on your wish list for a future birthday, anniversary or Christmas.

Much of the gear you'll need depends on how you plan to hunt antelope. If you'll be spending most of your time cruising in a pickup, glassing distant pronghorns from the vehicle, you'll need much less gear than if the success of your hunt depends on spending lots of time in a remote blind or covering lots of ground on foot. If your daily hunt begins with or includes considerable walking, the first thing you'll learn is to travel as lightly as possible, packing only those hunting accessories you absolutely need. When you're 4 or 5 miles from the truck, the last thing you want is a pack full of gadgets.

RIFLE SLING. One of the most important pieces of hunting gear a pronghorn shooter can own is a good rifle sling. First, a sling eliminates having to carry your rifle in your hands and makes a full day of packing the gun less fatiguing. Slings with the big, wide "cobra-style" pad make carrying the rifle even more comfortable. Many hunters, however, still prefer the military-type narrow slings that can be wrapped around the upper arm, locking the rifle into position for a much steadier hold than possible with the rifle held off-hand or even rested against the knees (below). One of the best slings on the market for this style of shooting is the Super Sling®, from the Outdoor Connection, Inc. With one hand you can quickly adjust the Super Sling® from the perfect length for carrying, to the perfect length for military-wrap shooting. The military wrap of the sling takes an extra few seconds of time, but if you've made a good stalk, the pronghorns shouldn't know you're around anyway.

RIFLE REST. Due to the long-range shooting usually required in antelope hunting, a solid hold or rest is vital to success. Many hunters now pack a set of the lightweight, often shock-corded, crossed shooting

Muzzleloader hunter using crossed shooting sticks

Train yourself to shoot accurately using the "military wrap" method. Start by wrapping your arm through the sling (inset) then grasp the gun's forearm while resting your elbow on your leg.

sticks. Other designs feature collapsible legs that can be quickly extended and adjusted for different heights. Several companies also offer a simple mono-type rest, some of which double as a walking stick, with one or more 2- to 3-inch-long shelves for resting the forearm of the rifle. The really serious antelope gun may feature a folding bipod that attaches directly to the forestock of the rifle, always handy for immediate use.

A good natural rest like a tree stump won't be found out on the prairie, and a light, portable rest such as those detailed here could mean the difference between making a 200-yard shot, or missing. Getting into a low sitting position, with the rifle rested in the crotch of a solid set of shooting sticks, will help combat the wind as well. When gusts climb up to 30 mph or more, it's nearly impossible to refine your hold on a distant buck if the wind is rocking you back and forth.

OPTICS. Never forget that the pronghorn has exceptional eyesight. Whether they actually have the 6-power or 8-power vision for which they are credited one thing is certain: if you're out in the open and if you can see a pronghorn, it's already spotted you. When going after an animal with such keen eyesight, the hunter should equip himself with good optics.

In the past, a spotting scope was so heavy and burdensome that you almost needed someone to tag along just to carry it on the hunt. Fortunately, today's compact models are very light, and when matched with a small folding tripod, they easily slip into a daypack with plenty of room left over. Due to the high magnification of these scopes, ranging from 18 or 20 power all the way up to 45, 60 or 80 power, the tripod is a must for a shake-free view of a pronghorn buck.

In addition to a spotting scope, you should carry a quality pair of binoculars. The movement of an antelope herd is more easily tracked through a set of 7- to 10-power binoculars than with a tripod-mounted spotting scope. Although a little on the heavy side, binoculars with large 45 to 50mm front lenses gather much more light than the 20 to 25mm front lenses found on compact binoculars. The additional light the front lenses allow in, plus the overall sharpness and clarity of top-quality binoculars, allows the hunter to spend more time glassing with less eye fatigue. Like spotting scopes, today's binoculars are noticeably lighter than past models.

Once you've located a good buck with your binoculars and have sized up the terrain separating you from him, take a much better look at him through the

Bushnell laser rangefinder

spotting scope. Make sure he's a "shooter" before you begin a stalk. Good optics can save you miles of boot leather.

Finally, never use the scope on your rifle to glass for antelope or to take a better look at what you think may be a distant buck. The hunter who uses his rifle scope in this manner will sooner or later break the cardinal rule of hunting: Never point your gun at something you don't intend to shoot. Sooner or later a hunter who glasses the landscape with his rifle scope will see another hunter. At that point, he's aiming his rifle at another human being. Don't Do It!

RANGEFINDERS. Other than a flat-shooting, deadly accurate centerfire rifle and matched ammunition, the greatest thing to come along for hunting pronghorns is the lightweight laser rangefinder.

Judging distance in wide-open country is tough. Even those who take pride in being right-on "most of the time" find that they can be off by a country mile occasionally, usually when attempting a shot on a trophy antelope buck. The truth is, most hunters are terrible judges of distance. And the relatively small size of a pronghorn, surrounded by miles and miles of nothing, compounds the problem. Even if the hunter misjudges the distance by only 50 yards, out at 300 yards that could easily mean a shot that strikes too high or too low.

Accurate to within a yard or two at 300 or 400 yards, today's rangefinders take all guessing out of the yardage. With some of the more popular models, like the Bushnell Yardage Pro, you sight in on a distant object and simply push a button. The yardage reading comes up instantly, and accurately.

Rangefinders have not only gotten better over the last decade or so, but they've also become more affordable.

You can buy a very reliable laser rangefinder for about $200. Less than a decade ago, you would have paid twice that amount for a rangefinder with far inferior capabilities.

Most of the early models depended on a reflective surface in order to get a reading. But other than the bright white rump hairs of a pronghorn, there are not many reflective surfaces in the sagebrush-covered terrain inhabited by antelope. Current models, however, are capable of reading the distances to just about any solid object, reflective or otherwise.

Many of the laser rangefinders available now are smaller and lighter than ever before. One compact model from Leica weighs just 10 ounces and measures

only 4x4x1 inches. It fits handily into the breast pocket of most jackets.

For hunters who don't have hundreds of dollars to spend on a laser rangefinder, there are still the more affordable split-image type units. These have been around for some time, and like virtually everything we now use, these too have been improved by modern technology. The hunter simply looks through the viewfinder, sights in on a distant object, and adjusts the top dial until the double images first observed come together as one. The yardage can then be easily read. A 400-yard split-image model can be accurate to within +/- 22 yards at 400 yards; a 1,000-yard model can be accurate to within +/- 30 yards at its farthest reading.

RIFLE SCOPE RANGEFINDERS. If your scope is equipped with a plex-type reticle, it can be used to give you a better idea of the distance to your target. First you have to determine the distance between the points of the heavy portion of the vertical reticle on a given power at a known distance. Take a piece of white poster board, then using a felt-tip pen draw a vertical line in the center with with hash marks every 4 inches that will be visible through the scope at 100 yards. Next, get back to exactly 100 yards, look through the scope and determine the distance between the points of the heavy, thicker portions of the plex reticle. With the magnification set at 9-power, the average distance from point to point is around 8 inches. Now, assuming that at 9-power you are looking at an average-sized prairie goat that's about 16 inches from withers to brisket, and if it fits perfectly between these points, you know that the antelope is somewhere around 200 yards away. If the animal only fills up half the plex area, say from the top of the bottom thicker portion to the juncture of the very fine crosshairs, then you know your target is out there at about 400 yards.

Some scopes have built-in grids for measuring distant targets. And while using the scope to measure a distant target is not as accurate as getting the range with a laser rangefinder, it's still more accurate than what most of us can estimate with the naked eye.

PACKS. Gather up enough stuff and you'll need a good pack. If you're traveling lightly, without a spotting scope or an extra jacket, then a fanny pack may be all you need. A good one will fit snugly around your waist and won't restrict your movement. Some of the more elaborate designs, built for packing quite a bit of stuff, feature shoulder straps to help carry the weight. However, if you're going to be packing that much stuff, you may want to invest in a good daypack. Most of these offer plenty of room for a good spotting scope and small tripod, an extra jacket, snacks or an entire lunch, and even lightweight rain gear. Small pockets on the outside make it easier to find smaller items, such as a compass, knife, candy bar or a folded topographical map. In a pinch, a well-stuffed daypack also makes a great rifle rest.

QUALITY DAYPACKS, such as this Master Guide Backpack from Crooked Horn Outfitters, are quiet, durable and waterproof.

Slick Shooting Sticks

I've never claimed to be a great offhand shot. In fact, I've never claimed to be a *good* offhand shot. Whenever possible, I go out of my way to find a rest of some sort to steady the rifle, even for a 100-yard shot. In antelope country there isn't much to choose from in the way of a rifle rest, and more often than not I'll simply make one by placing my hunting jacket over some sagebrush.

As for monopods, bipods, tripods or any other gizmo that screws or clamps onto a rifle, I find them bulky, awkward and always getting caught on something. And they add weight to the rifle. Sure, they'll definitely help steady a rifle for a long shot, and I just might use one if I could afford a gun bearer.

Several years ago, I learned about a slick trick that converts two aluminum arrows and the plastic top from a 35mm film canister into a handy, extremely light set of crossed shooting sticks. The arrangement is easily made by punching two closely spaced holes in the plastic top, then sliding in the arrows. The flex of the plastic film canister top allows the arrows to be pulled apart to form an "X" arrangement, providing a solid forearm rest for shooting from the sitting position. The plastic top can be quickly slid up or down on the arrow shafts, adjusting the height of the rest.

This is a great way to get additional mileage out of a couple of worn, damaged or slightly bent aluminum arrows. The homemade shooting sticks weigh practically nothing, and fold easily until you set them up for use.

- Don Oster

Pronghorn Hunting

Scouting

The most important part of any antelope hunt may be the time spent scouting for a particular buck or bucks in a certain size class. And as with most other big-game hunting, there is definitely a "home-court advantage" if you happen to live within reasonable driving distance of your hunting area. But, if you are like many pronghorn hunters who travel from out of state, spending much time in your hunting area prior to the season is probably out of the question. It then becomes something of a "scout as you go" proposition.

Even among hunters who live less than an hour or two from the hunting area, few actually spend much time scouting for antelope. This is especially true in really good pronghorn country, where the animals are almost always in sight. It's true that if antelope are in your designated hunting area, due to the open nature of their habitat, the animals aren't difficult to eventually locate. In fact, many pronghorns are taken on opening day of the season by hunters who never venture off of the dusty two-track roadways. However, these hunters are missing the real experience of pursuing antelope. Simply shooting a pronghorn buck that stands and watches the truck pull to within 100 to 200 yards is just that: shooting an antelope.

Early in the season, a good herd buck may strike a pose near a two-track, watch an approaching pickup

come to a stop and see a rifle barrel suddenly appear across the hood. Quite a few impressive bucks are taken in this manner. However, if it's a true trophy-class buck you're looking to hang on the wall, chances are good that it will require a bit more work than that. And even those easy goats, which allow vehicles to approach within rifle-shot distance on opening day, become an entirely different animal by the second morning. In other words, they catch on quickly. Usually by the end of the second day they have come to realize that stopped pickup trucks mean trouble. The big lucky buck that has had bullets whistle past his ears soon grows less tolerant of vehicles in his territory and becomes extremely wary. A seasoned 4- or 5-year-old trophy-class pronghorn buck becomes nearly impossible to approach; pressured even lightly, he will readily

vacate the area. In short, such bucks may give you only once chance.

If you have your sights set on taking a record-book-class buck, you have to hunt in an area where there are record-book bucks, and you must have these bucks on your hunting property. Your scouting may begin by looking through the Boone and Crockett or the Pope and Young record books to see where the highest number of record-book bucks have been taken. Keep in mind that your chances of taking a buck of this quality are slim if none or few have been taken from the area in the past.

Follow-up scouting includes determining the availability of permits and the actual hunting opportunities found in the area. If the region is made up primarily of privately owned properties, the hunter needs to contact landowners well before investing in the cost of applying for a permit. In many trophy antelope units, outfitters often have the best ranches leased. If so, and you still have your mind set on hunting the area, chances are you'll have to book with an outfitter. If the land is not leased by an outfitter, you'll probably be faced with paying an expensive access fee.

One advantage of hunting with a quality outfitter is that they should already have the best goats located by the time you arrive. If you're hunting on your own, especially in terrain you've never seen before, you could have your work cut out for you. Step one is getting to know the lay of the land. By first obtaining topographical maps, the pronghorn hunter can ascertain how much of the area is open to public hunting, and where the land is privately owned. Much of the best pronghorn range in the West is under the control of the Bureau of Land Management, and most of these millions of acres are open to public recreation, including hunting. Detailed maps are available of the different districts the BLM manages and normally cost only a few dollars each. Hunters can also visit www.terraserver.com on the Internet and print out topographical maps for most areas, and in some cases, find aerial photos of a particular hunting area.

Clearly mark the property lines on your maps. Nothing fouls up a hunt more quickly than a trespassing issue. Mark all roads, fence lines and stock-watering sources such as ponds or tanks. Talk to ranchers and ranch hands who regularly work in the area; they see game all the time. Usually they are more than willing to tell you about the locations where antelope herds have been regularly observed. Most of these cowboys are good game spotters and know a trophy antelope when they see one. You just might learn a lot about the number and quality of animals on a place before you ever hunt there.

PRONGHORN TRAILS are one of the most important pronghorn signs to find during a pre-hunt scouting trip. This is especially true for bow or muzzleloader hunters who want to build ground blinds and ambush pronghorns as they travel between bedding and feeding areas.

When you arrive at your hunting area, first take a tour of the place. When you see antelope, observe them from a distance. They can't read calendars and don't know that hunting season opens in a day or two. As you ease around the property in your pickup or SUV, you probably look like just another ranch worker making his rounds – as long as you don't attempt to get too close. If you need a better look at a buck, do it from a mile or so away through a powerful spotting scope. There is absolutely no sense in spooking antelope during pre-season or pre-hunt scouting trips.

Stop occasionally as you drive ranch roads to glass for antelope. Also, make note of high vantage points to use later as spotting locations. Be sure to visit each water source and look for pronghorn tracks along the edge of the water. Remember that pronghorns don't have dew claws, and may be sharing

many of these water holes with mule deer. When you locate a heavily used water source, look for the trails leading to it. If you are going to hunt with a bow or muzzleloader, this would be a fine time to look for potential places to set up a blind or build one from the brush growing in the area. Bowhunters shouldn't locate their blinds so close to a trail that it is impossible to bring the bow to full draw without being spotted. Often a blind that's 25 to 30 yards back is more effective than one 10 to 15 yards from the trail.

Heavily used trails should not be too difficult to find. Where cattle are grazed, there's a good chance the area will have fences. Follow a trail far enough in these areas and you're sure to find where the antelope cross under a fence. While a mile-long fence line may look exactly the same all along its length, pronghorns often cross under fences at only selected spots. Look for a worn or wallowed out spot under the fence and lots of broken hairs on the ground, plus a few clinging to the barbs of the bottom strand of fence. When you find such a crossing, you've also found another great spot to set up an ambush. If the crossing is along the property boundary line, hunting pressure on the neighboring property could make the crossing a hot spot. Other hunters could put a herd buck right in your lap. Just be sure to let him cross under the fence and onto your property before taking the shot.

During pre-season scouting, herds haven't been disturbed or hassled, and they go about their daily routines on a schedule that can almost be timed on a clock. After checking out the obvious places such as fence crossings and water holes, head for a high vantage point and be prepared to be patient. Get a comfortable place to lie in the grass, set up a spotting scope and be entertained by all of the antelope movement within sight. Note the patterns of each herd as it moves from bedding to feeding to watering areas. Although pronghorns do move around some after dark, a herd may habitually bed close to the same place each night. Note each movement along a trail or ground feature they use when feeding starts. Observe when and where they go to water, and note the intervals when the herd stops to rest and then move again. These patterns can be valuable when selecting an ambush site. A herd may go to an alfalfa field to feed at first light, move to a pond for water, then travel to a hillside to rest briefly before moving out to feed again. If undisturbed, the herd will repeat this pattern the next day, giving you an edge that can mean success.

If the antelope are beginning to show signs of rutting behavior, a herd buck will be one busy boy. He'll show impatience when trying to keep his does herded together and will hastily send visiting bachelor bucks on their way. The biggest herd buck and his harem should command most of your attention. Size this one up carefully, and mentally score his horns if you're interested in putting an animal in the record books. Once he has passed your inspection, make him your sole objective. Watch his every move and try to put together a pattern.

The beauty of antelope behavior is that you never become bored watching them. They never stay in one place for long. Their motors seem to be running at all times, and even at idle they're still moving and eating.

Once you've unraveled the herd buck's movement and daily routine through long-range scouting, you should have a good chance to take him during the hunt. There will probably be several options available for conducting a successful stalk or setting up an ambush. For instance, an alfalfa field where the antelope feed regularly may have a row of large round bales stored near one fence line. These make a great blind, especially if they're close to a gap in the fence or a fence crossing where a herd regularly enters the field to feed. Such a setup is a prime spot to hunt in the morning and evening. Likewise, the base of a windmill next to a water hole can be draped with camouflaged netting to create a perfect blind. And with a very flat-shooting centerfire rifle, the hunter who gets himself situated on a rise overlooking several trails may be in the right spot to get a crack at a trophy buck.

Unfortunately your scouting may reveal that the herds in your hunting area don't show any consistent patterns of movement. However, even when this is the case, you should learn the lay of the land and know some of the areas the pronghorns tend to frequent, even if not on a regular basis. Most importantly, by learning the terrain features of the area, you'll have a better idea of how to stalk pronghorns once you've located a shooter buck.

Most antelope hunters don't really target a specific buck. Most simply set their sights on getting a shot at a good buck, and any animal that meets a certain minimum size is fair game. Quite honestly, little time is normally spent in pre-season scouting. In Wyoming, where 100,000 or more pronghorn permits are issued annually, a high percentage of pronghorn hunters are non-residents. For the most part, they can't get in much pre-season scouting, other than maybe the day before the hunt begins. The majority of antelope hunters in this state, and elsewhere, are scouting and hunting simultaneously. And it all kicks off in the first light of opening day. However, the hunter who has spent time patterning his buck often has his trophy on the ground by the time other hunters even begin to put together a game plan.

One of the keys to effective scouting is to limit your intrusion in an area. Try to leave the herd no clues that you're poking around. If you're successful in not alerting the animals, you stand an excellent chance of taking the buck of your choice once the hunting season begins.

Once a buck's patterns have been defined, select the best possible ambush spot for opening morning. If a herd leaves a bedding area in an arroyo in early morning and routinely travels straight to a hayfield, a logical ambush point would be where they enter the field or along a primary trail leading to the food source. Later in the morning, a water hole or trails leading toward it may be the best places to wait in ambush.

It is much simpler to ambush a known buck using a known pattern, than to show up on opening day with hopes of spotting a good buck and then stalking him. After all, in an area where there's considerable hunting pressure, you may not be lucky enough to be the first hunter to try to stalk the area's best trophy.

Scouting Slipup

In most states, pronghorn seasons are generally at least 5 to 10 days long. This allows the hunter to spend the first day or two combining his scouting with hunting. However, in New Mexico, the gun season may last for only 2 days. This short season places a premium on the day or two spent prior to opening morning to look over the hunt area and the quality of bucks found there.

As you may know, New Mexico is noted for producing some exceptional pronghorn bucks. And there very well could be a Boone and Crockett qualifier on just about any ranch. But you need to know he's there before filling your tag with the first good buck that comes along.

I was on one of these 2-day jaunts a couple of years ago, and my schedule didn't allow for any scouting time. I showed up the night before the season opened, and immediately started hunting at daylight the next morning. The weather started out bad the first day, then looked even worse the second day. I finally slipped up on a decent buck and took him, figuring it was the best I could do considering the weather and the short season. Then, as we were hauling out my buck, "Mr. Big" appeared from out of nowhere. Had I known there was such a buck in the vicinity, I would have gladly spent the entire 2 days looking for him, even if it meant carrying home an unfilled tag.

- Don Oster

Dealing with the Weather

Whoever coined the phrase "In a New York minute!" to denote something that can turn around quickly apparently never visited Wyoming in the fall. Here, the weather can change so quickly, it can easily catch a hunter completely off guard during the course of a single morning or afternoon. The weather can be summer or early fall in the morning, then change to the dead of winter by mid-afternoon.

The weather is one factor that no one can do anything about. When it turns sour, the pronghorn hunter has to be prepared. As we discussed earlier in the chapter titled, "Clothing & Footwear," you have to pack the right clothes. In order to cope with temperatures that may range from 90 degrees down to below zero, you must have outer layers that can protect you from drenching thunderstorms or blinding blizzards. If you don't have the proper gear, your only choice is to stay in camp and wait for the weather to pass, which it may or may not do before your hunt is over!

Most September or even early October antelope hunts throughout the West take place during some of

the most pleasant weather of the year. Generally speaking, mornings start out in the upper 30s or lower 40s, warming quickly into the 50s by mid-morning, then topping out somewhere in the 60s or 70s. A light jacket during the first few hours can feel darn good, and when the sun begins to sink toward that western horizon in late afternoon, temperatures once again can begin to dip, often requiring that you slip on that same jacket.

And this is exactly the weather that can cause a hunter to mistakenly pack the wrong clothing. Say you've hunted the same ranch, during the same season, with the same beautiful weather for 3 or 4 consecutive years. When it's time to pack your bag and

leave the East, Midwest or South and head for the plains of central Wyoming for yet another antelope hunt, you may pack only what you would have needed last year, or the year before, when the weather was nice. Only this year, once you've already driven 1,000 or 1,500 miles from home, you discover opening day an entirely different situation with temperatures hovering right around zero, and a 40 mph wind. That nice light jacket and pants that worked so well on previous hunts suddenly isn't enough to keep you warm even in camp.

Anytime a fall hunt takes you into the plains that border the mountain regions of the West, always have stuffed away somewhere in your duffel bag a heavily insulated jacket, insulated underwear, maybe a set of insulated bibs, warm boots and heavy socks to go along with them. Remember, when it begins to get warm, you can always shed some of this clothing. But if it turns bitterly cold and snowy, and your warmest clothing happens to be thousands of miles away at home, you're going to experience one miserable outing – if you get out at all.

Wet weather, be it rain or snow, can really complicate an antelope hunt. Many of the simple two-track roadways cutting across much of today's pronghorn habitat are often barely passable during dry weather. Once drenched by hard rains or a wet snow, many become as slick as grease. Trying to negotiate a wet

two-track angling up a steep slope is simply asking for trouble. Hunting on foot when it's really muddy isn't much better. Where the soil has a clay or gumbo base, it can collect on your boots, adding pounds to each step. If the skies really open up and your hunting area is inundated by torrential rains, the antelope will commonly bunch up and hunker down, especially when the downpour is accompanied by strong winds. Soon you'll believe that the earth opened up and swallowed all of the animals you were hunting just prior to the storm.

Snow makes spotting distant antelope extremely difficult. The white rumps and lower body markings that made the animals easier to see among the dark clumps of sagebrush or open grass become a very effective snow camouflage pattern once the white stuff begins to blanket the ground and clings to much of the low brush. In fact, a motionless pronghorn standing only a hundred yards away is often totally undetectable until it moves.

Rain or shine, warm or cold, the one weather condition that every antelope hunter must learn to cope with is wind. Across the wide-open terrain the antelope calls home, seldom does it blow at less than 15 to 20 mph. Spending the entire day hunting in strong winds is physically tiring, but the real effect is usually seen in how it impacts your shooting. When hit by hard gusts of wind, the hunter simply cannot help but rock or shake from the sudden force. Shooting from the standing, kneeling or other upright position in heavy winds is extremely difficult. And when faced with shooting at 200 to 300 yards with a strong crosswind, chances are you'll have to figure in some good old "Kentucky Windage" to allow for bullet drift. And at the longer ranges, you may be surprised to discover that it could be one or more goat-lengths. Many excellent bow shooters have claimed that when attempting a 25-yard shot in a 20- to 30-mph crosswind, their arrows have blown so far off course they missed their targets by half an antelope body length.

When the wind really howls, the antelope may seem to totally disappear. Sight is the pronghorn's first line of defense against predators and other dangers. If the wind is constantly moving things around, detecting an unusual movement becomes increasingly difficult for the animals, and they grow more and more edgy. Often, they'll move into shallow depressions to escape strong winds, and may remain there until the winds subside. Where you once could glass and easily spot three or four different herds in short order, you may find the terrain seemingly free of antelope. These times can test both your will and game-spotting abilities to the fullest.

The White Wall

One Wyoming hunt years ago sticks in my mind about how quickly the weather can change on the prairie. Several hunting partners and I had driven out from Minnesota in early October. The weather was beautiful, and we spent several hours sizing up bucks as we drove across the first hundred miles of the state, headed for Cheyenne, where we planned to pick up groceries for a weeklong stay in antelope camp. None of us wore a jacket as we pulled into the parking lot of the supermarket and went inside to pick up provisions. The temperature was well into the mid-60s.

With enough grub to eat well for the next week, we headed north on a secondary highway out of Cheyenne. Forty miles from town, with the sun shining brightly on the truck, we came to a white wall of falling snow. We stopped less than a half-mile from the snow curtain and got out of the truck. It was still near 60 degrees. Thinking that the snow was simply a freak squall, we decided to drive on through, believing it would clear up a mile or two down the road. It didn't, and 10 miles later, I was barely able to turn the truck around and get the hell out of there. The snow was nearly a foot deep, and getting deeper by the minute.

Strangely, we drove back to approximately where we had stopped earlier, and the sun was shining once again. We backtracked several miles, then took the interstate north, thinking that we could get around the side of the snow squall. Again, this time about 40 miles north of Cheyenne, we hit the same front and managed to travel about 20 more miles before being forced off the highway to spend the night in a small roadside motel. The next morning, we were greeted by 15 inches of snow, 20-degree temperatures and the hardest antelope hunting I've ever experienced.

– Don Oster

Short 2- and 3-day hunts can be totally lost to several days of bad weather. Where the season length permits, always try to allow a minimum of 5 or 6 days for any antelope hunt. An extended period of rotten weather could force you to spend a good portion of that time sitting in camp. However, if you happen to be in antelope country once the weather breaks, you could be in for some of the best hunting of your life. Just like you, the pronghorns are happy to get out, and may move around more than normal. Also, if the weather kept you pinned down for 2 or 3 days, it probably did the same to other hunters in your area. After a few days of no pressure, you may find the pronghorns easier than ever to approach.

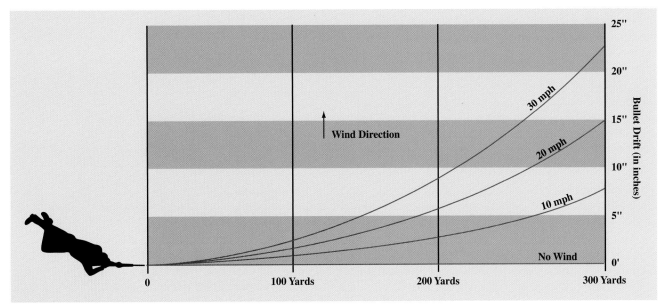

BULLET DRIFT increases as wind velocity and range increase. The chart shows how crosswinds of 10, 20, and 30 mph would affect the path of a .30-06, 150-grain bullet at 100, 200 and 300 yards. As the chart indicates, a 10-mph crosswind would cause the bullet to drift less than 1 inch at 100 yards. But in a 30-mph crosswind, the bullet would drift over 22 inches at 300 yards.

Winter Camping

As as antelope camps go, ours was pretty basic. We were hunting the high plains of west-central Wyoming, about 40 miles south of Pinedale. The region is an endless horizon of gently rolling ridge after gently rolling ridge, each heavily covered with sagebrush, and home to a healthy population of pronghorns. One spot in the huge 250,000-acre tract was just about as good as the next for pitching camp, with no location offering much protection from the constant wind. With that in mind, we set up camp right in the middle of the area where we had spotted the largest number of prairie goats.

Our two metal-framed canvas tents looked somewhat out of place in that sea of sagebrush, but at the end of a long day in steady 20- to 30-mph winds, those tents, cots and sleeping bags were as comfortable as home. This was the first antelope hunt for my two hunting partners, and they were having the times of their lives. Early the first morning, one of them scored on a decent buck, and 2 days later we were still trying to get the other a shot.

It was mid-September, and during the first 3 days the weather had been absolutely beautiful, with high blue skies and temperatures in the mid- to upper 60s. However, as we sat around the campfire that third night, waiting for a pot of pronghorn stew to cook a little longer, I noticed a heavy cloud bank cutting diagonally across the northwestern sky. The breeze that evening had a little more bite to it than the previous couple, and after watching the approaching front, I jokingly looked at my two companions and said, "Better enjoy the rest of summer, because I think winter gets here tomorrow."

Of course everyone laughed, but never in my life had I made a more accurate prediction. Sometime during the night, the wind picked up and the tents were flapping wildly at daybreak. As I unzipped the front flap, I was greeted by a blanket of white that covered everything in sight, and snowflakes as large as silver dollars continued to fly past horizontally. By noon the ground was covered with nearly 8 inches, and for the next 3 days the warmest it got was the upper 20s. We managed to fill all of our tags with reasonably good bucks, but by the time we broke camp that sixth evening, we were more than ready to leave. Our cozy little home on the range wasn't so cozy anymore.

– Toby Bridges

Spot & Stalk

One look out across the wide-open habitat of the pronghorn is all it takes to tell a hunter that here is an environment tailor-made for long-range glassing. At first glance, most of the terrain may seem far too open to provide much cover for the hunter attempting to sneak within a few hundred yards of an animal with such keen eyesight. However, careful examination usually begins to reveal slight rises in the terrain, deep breaks, arroyos and the occasional butte, all of which provide the opportunity for you to crawl, duck walk, slither, slide, crouch and scoot your way closer while remaining hidden from the pronghorns' watchful eyes. A difficult stalk on a wary pronghorn buck is a great test to anyone's hunting ability.

The traditional, most common and easily the most enjoyable way to hunt pronghorns is to locate them at long range, then use personal stealth to close in for a shot. For that reason the technique is often referred to as "glass and stalk" or "spot and stalk." One thing is certain: with a good set of binoculars or a powerful spotting scope, you can see forever and beyond. Provided there's no snow on the prairie, the white hair on a pronghorn, especially the rump, shows up clearly for miles, provided the antelope are up and about. As soon as they lie down in sagebrush or grass for a rest and cud-chewing session, they practically disappear and it will take sharp eyes and good optics to find them.

In top pronghorn country, the patient hunter with a good vantage point will glass numerous antelope during the course of a day. Because of the opportunity to look over lots of game before deciding which goat to take, the spot-and-stalk technique is the most widely used pronghorn hunting tactic. It generally accounts for upwards of 90 percent of all pronghorns harvested during any given year. The technique is a great way to look over lots of antelope, watch the animals as they go about their daily routines, and size up the horns of several bucks. When the hunter hasn't had the time to get in proper pre-season scouting, it could be called the "spot-and-scout-as-you-hunt"

technique. Those hunters who opt to shoot their bucks without ever leaving the two-track roads and their vehicles miss out on all of this fun.

During the rut, the hunter who spends time glassing may have the opportunity to witness one of the fastest high-speed chases in the world as a herd buck drives off bachelor invaders who try to steal the does from his harem. It's a busy time for the dominant buck, which must ward off male intruders while trying to keep his band of does together.

Although the buck is the objective of your hunting efforts, the sharp-eyed does are your real adversaries. They always seem to be on the lookout for danger, and they exhibit more than their share of curiosity. Compounding the problem is that you may have to pull off an error-free stalk under the scrutiny of a dozen or more does. And if just one of them catches a glimpse of your belly crawling through sparse cover, there's a very good chance that the herd won't be anywhere in sight the next time you take a peek.

Spot-and-stalk hunting requires mobility. To properly view the surrounding territory, you must move to a high vantage point. To cover the maximum amount of real estate in the least amount of time, most hunters use vehicles to reach their different spotting locations. To keep from spooking animals that may be nearby, the pickup or all-terrain vehicle should be kept back from the summit. Then,

on foot, the hunter should ease out onto the highest point from which he can set up and glass a large expanse of open range.

SPOT-AND-STALK OPTICS. Top-quality 7- to 10-power binoculars are ideal for scanning a huge expanse for herds or single bachelor bucks on the prowl. Once you've spotted a buck, it's time to take a better look at him, and that's done a lot more easily with a tripod-mounted 30- to 60-power spotting scope. Even if you could obtain a set of binoculars with sufficient magnification to properly judge a buck that's a mile or more away, chances are you wouldn't be able to hold them steady enough to see clearly.

Most experienced antelope hunters rely heavily on the use of both a set of crisp, clear binoculars for first locating antelope, then a variable-power spotting scope for zooming in on a buck. When the magnification of the optics you use gets above 10 or 12 power, the use of a tripod is mandatory. Many of the modern spotting scopes now available come with a small, folding tripod, making these scopes compact and easy to carry.

Any hunter looking to outfit himself just for pronghorn hunting will find that a premium quality set of binoculars and spotting scope represents a major expenditure. Some of the very best binoculars with top-quality glass can set you back over $1,000, and a top-of-the-line spotting scope can be even more expensive. The beginning

pronghorn hunter will probably choose lower-cost optics. As a rule, a good, functional pair of binoculars can be bought for $200 to $400. The price range is about the same for a functional spotting scope with variable magnification ranging from 20 up to 60 or more power.

So, what is the difference between a $200 pair of 10-power binoculars and $1,500 binoculars of the same magnification? It's the quality of the glass. All you have to do is spend a day peering through a true world-class pair of binoculars and anything less will, from that time on, seem blurry and slightly out of focus. If at the end of a 12-hour day spent glassing the prairie you have a splitting headache, you need to invest in better optics. They impose far less strain on your eyes.

If there aren't enough two-track roads to provide access to all of your hunting area, or if you experience a couple of days with hard rain or snow, you'll come to appreciate quality, lightweight optics even more. When it gets wet, prairie soil can get so slick that any vehicle becomes almost worthless, even a four-wheel drive. Faced with wet, impassable roads, or no roads at all, the pronghorn hunter may find that it's time to use a little boot leather. Now, this is *real* antelope hunting, and any buck taken will be a buck earned. Walking in those expanses makes you really scan the terrain to save steps. You'll learn to use all terrain breaks to reach vantage points for glassing. Antelope are not all that accustomed to seeing humans on foot in their domain. If you are spotted, your upright form instantly stands out as different to them, and they'll probably run off into the next county.

GLASSING TIPS

Pronghorn hunters tend to be a curious lot. They always have to know what's over the next rise. Depending on the situation or the lay of the land, this trait can be either good or bad. On the positive side is that it may be enough of an incentive to get a hunter to walk to a new vantage point from which he can look over a more productive area. On the negative side is that the strong lure to abandon one spotting location for another may find the hunter either on the move or absent when a true trophy buck moves through the original area. But that's pronghorn hunting. Being in the right spot and having the confidence to stick with the spot comes from proper pre-season scouting, plus knowledge of the area and antelope movement within that area.

Patience is a virtue when it comes to antelope hunting. If all of your pre-hunt efforts tell you that a good

buck regularly frequents one part of your hunting area, then the longer you stay in one good glassing location with a good view of the area, the greater your chances of locating that buck again. The key is to be on a high ridge, mesa, butte or hill where you can settle down with binoculars and spotting scope, then spend the morning, afternoon or entire day carefully glassing every inch of the terrain in the surrounding area. In order to see down into small arroyos, ravines or other terrain breaks, you may have to shift your glassing position several hundred yards, or maybe a quarter to a half-mile in one direction or the other in order to glass these areas.

Many veteran spot-and-stalk hunters cover the areas around them in something of a grid pattern, glassing back and forth slowly from one landmark to another, then doing the same thing again, only concentrating on terrain either slightly closer or slightly farther away. By sectioning the area they are watching, and spending equal time on each section, or grid, they properly glass everything.

Antelope have a habit of appearing from out of nowhere. A hunter can sit and glass for hours, covering over and over the same seemingly empty terrain, and then suddenly a herd of antelope is standing right out in the open. It's as if they climbed out of a hole in the ground. And in a sense, they probably did just that. Terrain that seems nearly flat and open can hide depressions, nearly undetectable rolls, obscured arroyos or other topographical changes that can keep an entire herd of antelope out of sight for hours. During midday, it's not uncommon for a herd, watered and with bellies full, to find a nice out-of-the-wind spot to lie down and rest for several hours or more. If that spot just happens to be on the other side of a slight rise or ridge, a hunter could sit on higher ground and glass for a couple of hours and not see an single antelope, even though a herd could be less than a half-mile away. Then, bingo, they rise and walk out into the open, many times catching the hunter completely off guard. That is, if he hasn't already grabbed up all his gear and headed off to another piece of high ground from which to glass. Many times you cannot glass carefully or long enough.

Obviously, moving and feeding antelope are the easiest to spot. One thing that works to the hunter's advantage is that antelope are seldom still for any great length of time. Their nervous behavior dictates that they lie down for only short periods, then rise to feed or move to another location. The ideal scenario is to spot a resting herd, and then put a stalk into motion. The main problem with trying to stalk a moving herd is that in addition to keeping out of sight, the hunter must also anticipate the direction of the herd's movement. There's nothing more embarrassing or

LOOK for pronghorns all across the prairie. If you glass too much property too quickly, you'll probably miss seeing the animals that are bedded in or near some type of cover.

frustrating than to pull off a flawless stalk, keeping well down and out of sight, only to discover that the herd has turned and moved in another direction while you were crawling down a draw in the direction you thought they were headed.

STALKING TIPS

Once you've spotted a buck that meets all of your requirements, step one is to slip closer for a better look. Mentally map out a route, using any feature or terrain breaks that offer cover from those sharp antelope eyes as you approach the herd. Reference the stalk route by any prominent features such as a tree, ridge, rocks, ravine, etc. Count the number of draws, ridges or other features that must be crossed during the stalk. Everything will look different as you progress. These reference points will help keep you on course. If a herd is bedded, reference the spot to a ground feature. If the herd is moving, determine its direction of travel and plan your stalk to a place where you can intercept the antelope.

When stalking, stay completely out of sight of the herd whenever possible. Move along ravines, in creek beds, through tall sagebrush, or behind ridges. Use any terrain feature for concealment that leads you closer to the animals. Never move along a skyline. The pronghorn's keen eyesight can spot a moving hunter at amazingly long distances. It is very frustrating to peek over what should be the final rise to find no pronghorns in sight. Check reference points to see if you're still on course. The animals may have moved off, or you may have miscounted the number of ridges or draws between where you last saw the antelope and the high point from which you had been glassing. Carefully crawl to the nearest high point and glass again for the herd.

Provided the antelope are where you last saw them, you may want to consider taking a better look at the buck once you close the distance to 400 or so yards. Continue to remain hidden and ease up to a rise or to heavy ground cover that will allow you to glass or spot the buck to determine if he's really a shooter. Most good 10-power binoculars allow you to see the horns well enough from that distance to assess whether they have the height, mass and prong length to meet your requirements. (Refer to the measurement references found in the chapter, "Field-Judging Pronghorns.") If the buck doesn't, then there's no sense in devoting valuable hunting time to a stalk when you have no intention of taking the shot. If the buck is definitely a shooter, then continue the stalk through the final phase.

The hunter who finds that his initial stalk easily brings him within the effective range of his rifle and shooting ability may consider himself lucky. However, he'll miss the real essence of a pronghorn stalk unless it involves some crawling. The final stages of a typical stalk on antelope likely includes inching along on your hands and knees, or even belly crawling, in the sage or grass. Along the way you're sure to have plenty of unpleasant encounters with prickly little cacti and sharp shale rocks. Veteran antelope hunters who have experienced all of this in the past often use heavy knee and elbow pads, plus a pair of heavy leather gloves for protection from a variety of sharp, pointy things. It can take a month or more before some cactus spines fester enough to surface so they can be plucked from your hide.

The pronghorn hunter who covers a lot of ground on foot, and especially the hunter faced with a long stalk, can run into another hazard – rattlesnakes! This is particularly true during the early August and September hunts, before cold weather has sent the snakes into hibernation. There is no denying that the little prairie rattlers can put some spice into the hunt. To avoid a snake encounter, you need to be watchful and deliberate, giving a rattler plenty of time to set off his warning

buzz. Good snake boots can give you peace of mind, but the best course is to avoid contact altogether.

Grasshoppers will also keep your nerves on edge by doing a great rattlesnake buzz imitation when their wings rattle every time they take to flight. Still, as you ease across the open terrain, you must pay attention to every rattling sound. The next one could be the real thing.

An archery or muzzleloader hunter who has spotted a good buck and crawled to within a few hundred yards of it, may need to employ other tactics such as decoying or calling to lure it within shooting range. In contrast, a rifle hunter with a good scope and flat-shooting centerfire rifle may need to stalk to within only 300 yards or so of the buck. Still, always get as close as possible to the target without taking unnecessary risks that might spook the herd. Some of the most exciting antelope hunts occur when a stalk route gets you nearly face to face with a good buck.

MAKING THE SHOT

Barring any unexpected interruptions by other hunters or challenging bucks, a well-executed stalk should result in a decent shot at a standing animal. The rifle shooter should be able to stalk within his confidence range, then have plenty of time to slip into his rifle sling or set up to use any shooting aids. *Never* allow yourself to be tempted to take shots beyond the effective range of your rifle, or beyond your own shooting ability. *Never* try to make a shot on an antelope that's farther away than you've ever fired your rifle on a target. A pronghorn's body does not offer a particularly large target. It is much better to pass on a shot than risk wounding an animal. Unless he is unduly harassed, a buck usually remains in his territory. Whenever you pass a shot for any reason, it is

CRAWL with your eyes up and your butt down. Stop immediately if you spot a pronghorn looking your direction.

time to be patient. Watch the buck from a distance. You can be sure he and the herd will begin moving again within a short time and possibly toward a place that offers good conditions for a successful stalk.

Range estimation is difficult in flat plains country or across the open expanse of a ravine or arroyo. A reliable rangefinder, or a scope that allows the hunter to use the reticle to estimate range, is a valuable asset. Delivering a shot into the vital area of a pronghorn requires hitting within an 8- to 10-inch square. Making the shot should be the easiest part of the hunt, provided you have done a good job sighting in the rifle and you've spent sufficient time on the range to familiarize yourself with the ballistics and trajectory of your cartridge. The final steps of any spot-and-stalk gun hunt are to get a solid rest, calm yourself, make sure of your target, then gently squeeze off the shot.

CONCENTRATE before squeezing the trigger. It's common to be breathing hard after a long and difficult stalk, so make sure you've got control over your breathing before attempting the shot.

Lost in the Grass

Every pronghorn hunter loves to show off his stalking abilities when there's someone there to watch. And I must confess, I'm just as guilty as the next guy.

Several years ago, I had the opportunity to take renowned outdoor writer Tom McIntyre on his first muzzleloading antelope hunt. During some pretty extensive pre-season scouting of several ranches 25 miles west of Gillette, Wyoming, I located a 500-acre hayfield that often attracted five or six different herds each day. Several of the better bucks tended to hang close to a small pond near the center of the field, while one really good buck kept his does up on a higher section of the field, near a fenced-in pile of cut hay. I placed Tom near the water hole, while I settled into a comfortable blind at the base of the haystack.

All morning long I watched a handsome, straight-horned 14-inch buck feed and lounge around with his does about a quarter mile from my blind. Finally, I couldn't take it any longer. I crawled out the back of the blind, around the haystack and slithered down into a shallow draw that allowed me to move around the side of the ridge out of the pronghorn's sight. Fifteen minutes later, I bellied up to a barbed-wire fence 300 yards from the antelope, crawled under the bottom strand, took a course on the half-bedded herd and began to ever-so-slowly crawl through the nearly knee-high dry grass.

I dared not raise my head, knowing that I would be instantly spotted. Instead I just kept crawling and crawling and crawling, until I got to where I felt I would be within a hundred yards of the goats. My head inched upwards until my eyes cleared the grass.

There was nothing but a sea of waving grass in front of me, right where the antelope should have been. I began to wonder where they had gone when a sharp snort-wheeze-whistle right behind me caused me to instantly freeze. Slowly, I turned my head and was startled to see all 14 or 15 pronghorns standing just 30 yards away – behind me!

In a stiff-legged, yet graceful fast walk, the antelope moved another 75 or 80 yards off, then turned and stood to look back. By that time, I had rolled over into the sitting position and had the scope on my .50-caliber in-line muzzleloader centered on the buck. My thrilling stalk ended with a fine buck.

When I joined my hunting partner for a bite of lunch an hour later, he commented: "I thought that was darn clever crawling through that herd the way you did, then taking a shot from the back side. A very unusual, but apparently effective technique."

- Toby Bridges

Hunting from Blinds

The pronghorn's daily routine is one of movement. While the animals may frequently take short rest periods, most of the day is spent on the move feeding, running and playing, and going through the fall rutting rituals. But of all their daily movement patterns, one is constant: antelope need water and they'll go to a reliable water source at least once each day.

Fortunately for the hunter, the pronghorn seasons in most states take place during one of the driest periods of the year. Late summer and early fall in antelope country is usually a dry time, and water is often in short supply. Gone are most of the secondary water sources like shallow basins, which collect spring and early summer rain water, and the small streams flowing in some of the deep ravines during wet weather. For this reason, every well-established territory of a dominant buck will nearly always contain a reliable water supply in the form of stock ponds, active streams or stock watering tanks. These watering places are the key to a herd's location at one time or another during the course of each day.

When hunting pronghorn habitat for the first time, the hunter is wise to devote as much time as it takes to identify water sources. While feeding routines may change slightly from time to time, primary water sources generally remain the same, and the dominant buck of an area seldom wanders more than a mile or two from these spots.

To identify the most heavily used water sources, scout around ponds or stock watering facilities for antelope tracks. However, always remember this simple rule: *Never* run antelope away from a watering place. If you spot a herd at or near a water hole, stop, turn around and move away until you are far enough from them to prevent spooking the herd. Then check out the herd buck through a good set of binoculars or a spotting scope. Once you've found a herd that moves to a particular watering hole on a regular basis, you've found an ideal location for a blind.

In really arid country, a major water source that's the only water for miles may be on the territory boundaries of two, three or even four or more dominant bucks. If you're lucky enough to find such a situation, you can be assured that several herds may visit the same watering place at various times during the course of a single day. Where you know several herds are using the same water source, you are wise to hold off from shooting the first buck that shows up, unless it is a real bruiser. Because it's the only reliable water source for miles, bachelor bucks may pop up all day long in route to get their daily drink of water. In some areas, major water holes serve a hundred or more antelope on a day-to-day basis, giving the patient hunter opportunities at a half-dozen or more bucks on any given day.

Finding a suitable blind or stand location is not difficult for the patient centerfire-rifle hunter, provided you've located a primary watering area and have identified the trails leading to it. In fact, the setup for a rifle hunter may not require a blind at all. Concealment in a wash, or along a nearby ridge or point within 200 yards of where the antelope are headed, should be sufficient. Of course, bow and

muzzleloader hunters must get much closer, so a blind of some type is necessary.

It stands to reason that the best location for a blind is close to a main feeder trail leading to the water source, or within range of the water source itself. Sometimes the base of a windmill adjacent to a water hole can be brushed or covered with camouflaged netting to construct a roomy, comfortable blind. Outfitters catering to bowhunters often enclose the bottom 5 or 6 feet of a windmill base with olive- or tan-colored canvas months ahead of the season, giving the antelope plenty of time to adjust to a material that they cannot see through. And where the life-giving water simply comes up

out of the ground thanks to a submersible pump, hunters might even build a permanent blind or a canvas tent-like arrangement that pronghorns accept as natural after some period of time. These blinds often feature narrow open windows on each side, providing a portal to shoot through.

Less sophisticated blinds can be easily built by chopping sagebrush and piling it around the base of a windmill, using camouflaged netting stretched between poles driven into the ground, or maybe even taking the time to dig a 3- or 4-foot-deep pit and ringing it with a little extra brush. Anything that blends into the natural surroundings and provides concealment can be effectively used to hide the hunter from a pronghorn's unforgiving eyes. If you choose to dig and use a ground pit, make sure the landowner doesn't object. If you're on public property, make sure it's legal. Be sure to fill in the hole at the end of your hunt.

A long wait at a water hole with no action can suddenly get very interesting during the rut should two separate herds arrive at about the same time. Each herd buck will try to keep his group of does away from the other herd, while the ever-present bachelor hustlers add to the confusion. The hunter will find that he can go from no antelope to too many antelope in a very short time. However, the hunter who maintains his composure in the midst of such a situation will find that he has the advantage of a close-up comparison of several different bucks. This way he can pick the best on which to hang his tag.

While some of the more productive blinds are located near a well-used water source, other locations can produce a good buck for the hunter occupying a blind. One spot is where a heavily used pronghorn trail crosses under a fence. Often two or three trails will come together at a heavily used crossing, funneling lots of antelope movement through one location. These different trails may be links leading to or from prime feeding, bedding or watering places. While miles and miles of fence may look exactly the same to you, the antelope will nearly always choose one particular spot for crossing under a fence line. They'll travel well out of their way to cross under at that exact spot.

Prime fence crossings are easily identified by all of the hair on the ground and clinging to the barbs of the bottom strand of wire. Antelope hair rubs out or breaks off easily, making a frequently used crossing very obvious. Interestingly enough, a few "antelope-friendly" landowners have begun stretching a smooth, barbless bottom strand of wire, making it easier for pronghorns to cross under. Another sign that a crossing is well-used is a deep notch worn into the ground where the antelope repeatedly crawl beneath the bottom strand of fence.

Again, the hunter carrying a centerfire rifle won't have to place a blind right on the crossing, and he'll often be less detectable if it's located a hundred or more yards from where the antelope cross. The muzzleloading hunter may have to move in a little closer, while the archer probably wants to be well within 30 yards of the crossing. No matter what type of firearm you're hunting with, always position the blind so that it's downwind of the crossing. Many times you'll find a great fence crossing with very little, if any, cover nearby. This is where a pit blind can be deadly because it gets the hunter down at ground level.

A great way to build a blind along a fence is to place a temporary fence post 4 or 5 feet off to the side of one of the permanent fence posts. Then stretch heavy camouflaged netting along the fence and around your new post to create an effective triangular blind. Just be sure to use heavy netting, such as the military surplus type, which does not flap a lot in the wind. Any blind material moving too much may spook the normally nervous antelope.

Even if you locate a well-worn crossing beneath a fence, check it closely for fresh tracks to make sure it's currently in use. Antelope often shift movement seasonally within their territory, and may not have used a particular crossing for months. This is where good scouting of the hunting area the week or so before the season really pays off. Before establishing a blind site, you should already know the daily herd movement and use of the crossing when the herd moves to or from feeding and watering places. When spooked, antelope also use these crossings as escape routes, and you may find yourself in a pronghorn stampede. Normally, the hole under the fence is small and the animals cross under just one at a time. You may get a clear shot at the buck as he hesitates momentarily before passing through the opening. However, if the antelope are fleeing from something, once the pronghorns are on the other side, they'll go from 0 to 60 mph in a quarter-mile or less.

A hay or grain field can prove to be a food magnet that draws pronghorns on a daily basis. Remember, unless they're pressured, antelope adhere to a fairly strict routine. Your scouting should let you know the best times to hunt a field. While antelope may move to a field at just about any time of the day, you can

PORTABLE BLINDS, such as the model above from Double Bull Archery, are compact for easy carrying and set up in less than a minute. They're ideal for bow and muzzleloader hunters wanting to ambush pronghorns near water holes, fence crossings or along trails.

PERMANENT GROUND BLINDS are an inexpensive alternative to manufactured portable blinds. It may take several hours to construct such a blind, but once they're completed they offer excellent concealment from the watchful eyes of a pronghorn.

bet that they do so day in and day out at about the same time. If you find out that a herd moves into one of these fields in mid-afternoon, there's not much sense being there at daybreak. Take that time to hunt a more productive morning spot.

Pronghorns moving to feed in a hay or grain crop field will normally use the same avenue of approach each time. The ideal setup is a row of big round hay bales a hundred or so yards downwind from where the antelope enter the field. Of course, the bowhunter has to be closer, so a blind of some sort will probably be required.

If a herd uses an approach that keeps them out of range of the rifle, muzzleloader or bow you're using, you may want to consider making the "challenge" call. If you're bow or muzzleloader hunting, you may even want to consider using a decoy. Check out how to use these techniques in the decoying and calling chapter (p. 98) of this book.

No matter where you set up or what type of blind you use, set it up so you can be comfortable during a potentially long wait. You may have scouted well

Three for Three

There are times when nothing seems to go right for an antelope guide. You get busted by pronghorns on every stalk you try to pull off, the best blind locations are useless because the normally predominant northwest wind suddenly decides to blow from the southeast for a few days, or you simply end up with a client who can't hit anything with his $3,000 "Super Wampum Magnum" rifle. Those are the days you try to forget. The ones you always want to remember are when everything goes right.

I remember one such day in north-central Wyoming. I'd taken my vacation in order to guide for Lone Wolf Outfitters (of Buffalo, WY) and my first three clients were bowhunters looking to take their very first archery antelope. Accompanied by another guide, I took the trio to a sizeable ranch where we had identified at least a dozen different herds, and herd bucks. In the dim light of dawn, we placed our first hunter in a blind at the base of a windmill, 20 yards from where the antelope normally watered. About 20 minutes later, we had our second hunter in position in a blind built next to a cattle-watering pond fed by an artesian well. Our third hunter settled into a pit blind close to a very heavily used fence crossing not more than 15 minutes later.

My partner and I decided to drive to a high overlook and watch the pronghorn movement below. As soon as I nosed the old Suburban up to the crest and pulled out my binoculars, I immediately spotted our first hunter a mile away frantically waving his arms. As I looked around inside of the truck, I commented, "What the hell did he forget?"

We drove back down and discovered that he had already arrowed a nice buck. We quickly field-dressed the antelope and placed it in the back of the vehicle. Then, as we drove back out onto the road, we met the last hunter we set out. He too had taken a good buck. It had already been one heck of a morning. However, just 2 hours later, our third bowhunter made a perfect hit on his buck.

We were back at camp well before noon, with three Pope-and-Young-class bucks. Not bad for a few hours of stand hunting from ground blinds.

- Toby Bridges

enough to establish that a herd comes to feed or water during the early morning hours, but find that due to some other influence, such as hunting pressure, the antelope have changed to an evening visit. A comfortable stool or pad to sit on, some food and drinks in a cooler, and perhaps some good reading material make a long wait for the herd much more enjoyable.

Decoying & Calling

Whether or not you bow hunt, you have to applaud the determination and optimism of the archer who crawls through the sagebrush, grass and cactus toward a distant herd of antelope with the expectation of getting within reasonable bow range. As impossible as it may seem to get within 30 yards of the ever-watchful pronghorns, the bow-toting hunter who pulls it off and gets that close without being spotted has only accomplished half the feat. Now he must bring the bow to full draw and carefully aim before a buck reacts to the hunter's sudden appearance and bolts. And even if this is accomplished, there is always the chance that the antelope will react to the sound of the bow or bowstring and quickly turn or run just as the arrow is arriving.

Any way you look at it, the deck seems to be stacked against the bowhunter looking to score on a pronghorn.

Hunter drawing his bow over a Dutton Decoy (left)

Where It All Began

I think decoying antelope started a long time ago, as a spin-off from the technique of flagging them with a rag tied to a stick. The first time I became aware of the actual decoying technique was when my high school principal used a mounted pronghorn head as a decoy. An avid bowhunter, he still holds the South Dakota record for the largest pronghorn killed with bow and arrow.

I started experimenting with decoying by setting up in a field where antelope were coming to feed. I would place a homemade decoy and build a blind nearby with hay bales. Like hunting near a waterhole, it was a waiting game requiring too much patience. I did, however, enjoy moderate success with the decoy. These early experiences were the start of an evolution toward making the decoy portable and taking it to the pronghorn.

Decoying has worked well as an antelope magnet, especially during the rut. And combining calling with the decoy has doubled the effectiveness of the technique.

– Mel Dutton

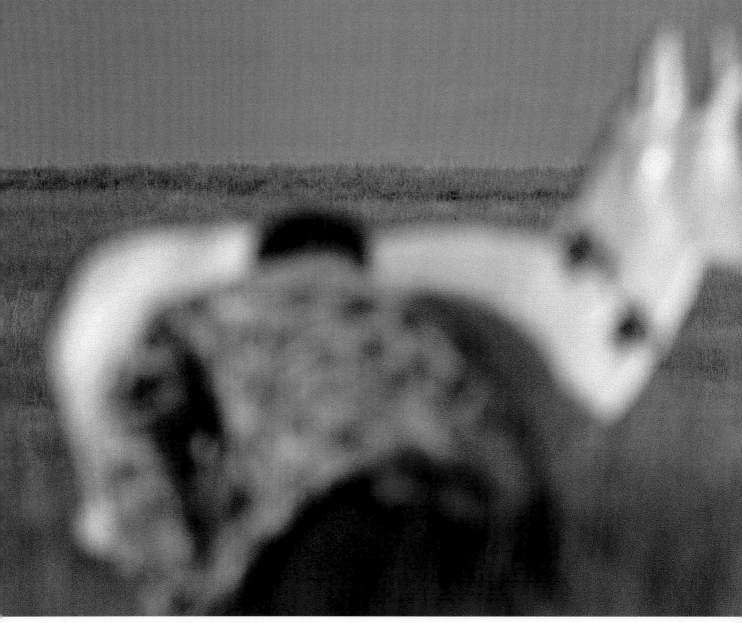

HIDE behind the Dutton Decoy, and be ready to draw your bow in an instant. Once a herd buck sees the decoy and hears the challenge call, he could close the distance in only a few seconds.

However, more and more bowhunters are doing just that each fall. Sure, a few go the "super stealth" route and belly-crawl their way into range, but most have learned to set up proper ambush sites near food or water sources. And some creative bowhunters are using a couple of newly developed pronghorn techniques, namely decoying and calling. The following paragraphs explain how you can succeed using these extremely productive and exciting methods.

DECOYING

Picture the following scenario:

Exhausted, with heart pounding from a torturous belly-crawl across a quarter-mile of hide-abrading lava rock and flesh-piercing cactus, you finally reach the top of the last rise and look down on a herd of pronghorns. The buck is definitely a good one, and

you decide to attempt getting the buck to come closer for a shot with your bow. You ready the bow that's laying on the ground next to you by placing a broadhead-tipped arrow on the string. Then, you unfold a lightweight, hinged buck antelope decoy and set it up by firmly planting the long, steel decoy stake into the ground. You immediately swivel the decoy so it's perfectly broadside to the herd, then crouch behind it. A peephole through the flat decoy silhouette allows you to watch the herd's reaction. You notice that they're all looking your way, so you place a game call to your lips and blow a challenge call to the herd buck.

The rut is in full swing, and bachelor bucks have been giving the herd buck fits. For several days they have been trying to steal some of his does, and he's done his best to keep them away. Now this strange buck (decoy) suddenly appears and has the gall to

The antelope suddenly runs in at full speed. You move back a yard or so from the backside of the decoy, pick up your bow and get ready for a shot. As the antelope approaches the 40-yard mark, you bring your bow to full draw, trying to remain as low as possible behind the decoy. The trophy is now at less than 30 yards. He comes to a screeching halt, and you inch up just far enough so the arrow clears the back of the decoy. Taking careful aim, you unleash the arrow. The shot is true, and the buck travels only 125 yards. You look to the heavens and thank God for making pronghorns.

Sounds exciting, doesn't it? Well, bowhunters who have successfully used the tactic say there's nothing like watching a fine trophy pronghorn buck charge in, hellbent for a fight. While the Plains Indians are known to have lured the curious antelope to within bow range using animal hides for disguise, the use of actual pronghorn decoys is a recently developed technique.

The decoys that give today's bowhunter a real edge were pioneered by South Dakota bowhunter Mel Dutton. He discovered the effectiveness of a decoy to attract pronghorn bucks in his high school days. In the years since, Mel has refined decoying to a finely honed success strategy for taking big antelope bucks. Realizing that he was onto something that would revolutionize bowhunting for antelope,

enter his territory to directly challenge him for breeding rights to the harem. From the dominant buck's perspective, this is the last straw.

The buck charges toward the trespasser in a stiff-legged gallop, extending his neck and body hairs to look bigger and more menacing. This 4-year-old dominant buck is in his prime. His horns are more than 15 inches in length, and he stops and begins shaking his impressive head gear back and forth at the intruder, then advances closer. But the strange buck (decoy) on the skyline stands its ground rather than depart at full speed as had all the other rival bucks. Maybe this one will take a little more urging or an outright fight before he leaves to torment some other distant herd buck.

MEL DUTTON pioneered the use of two-dimensional pronghorn decoys to attract herd bucks within bow range.

Was That a Bird?

For years I heard the funny birdlike sounds when I was antelope hunting. Never guessing that antelope were responsible for the noises, I dismissed them as the call of some strange winged creature. The sound was like a raspy bark, followed by a sort of rhythmic chuckling. It was several years before I was close enough to a pronghorn buck to actually see and hear him make the challenge sounds. Turns out that bucks and does frequently make snorting noises at each other. Some folks think the single snort is a warning, but I've observed that they will make the sound when they are not alarmed at all.

The most important vocalization from bucks is the challenge-snort sequence. The noise is made during the rut by one buck challenging the other over breeding rights to a harem of does.

This sound is a raspy snort, followed by a "ta…ta…ta…ta…ta" chuckle. I learned to make the sound with my mouth and used this challenge call in conjunction with decoying. The combination of decoying and calling has helped me bring numerous good herd bucks into bow range over the years. Recently, I worked with Brad Harris, of Lohman Calls, who developed and sells the challenge call commercially. It's easy to learn to use and can really bring a herd buck running and ready to fight. Nowadays the only problem you have is putting up with the laughter and strange looks you'll get when you tell ranchers or old-timers that you're going to call up some antelope. It may take a few years for them to learn that decoying and calling is a deadly combination for trophy goats.

- Mel Dutton

Dutton began producing light, easy to carry and quick to set up decoys for antelope. He also went on to produce similar decoy types for hunting other big game. His name has become synonymous with successful pronghorn bowhunting.

This technique has become a "must use" strategy for any serious bowhunter looking to hunt dominant herd bucks. It works best during the rut, when frazzled bucks are defending their territory, and the does they've gathered, against all comers. At this time, the herd bucks, which usually sport the best horns, are vulnerable because they'll readily approach an intruder and fight if necessary to chase him away.

Normally, the dominant buck pulls up 20 to 40 yards short of the decoy to size up his adversary before committing to an all-out fight. This is when the bowhunter often gets his best opportunity to get off a shot. But some decoying encounters get a little too close for comfort, and the hunter never gets off a shot because the buck runs full-tilt up to the decoy without stopping. These encounters usually end with the hunter spooking the oncoming buck at close range.

Decoying is usually done with a single buck decoy. However, there are times when the combination of a buck and a doe decoy seem to be more effective. Experienced bowhunters who rely on the use of decoys claim that the sight of a buck with a doe may send the message to the herd buck that the intruder has already hustled one of the does from his harem. The herd buck often rushes right in to reclaim her. In addition, the use of two decoys permits two hunters to participate in the hunt, doubling the chances for one person to get a good shot. This setup also allows one hunter to be the designated shooter while the other handles the calling.

The bowhunter should watch the approaching buck through a peephole in the decoy, or by peeking around either end of the decoy, making sure to keep his head below the decoy's back. Once he knows the buck is on its way, it's crucial that the hunter back away from the decoy a yard or so to ensure free movement of the bow and arrow tip. This ensures that the broadhead does not hit the back of the decoy when the hunter rises up to shoot. To keep from being spotted too soon, the hunter should bring his bow to full draw, if at all possible, while still crouched behind the decoy. Avoid trying to take a last-minute look at the antelope as it approaches. Remain hidden behind the decoy until it's time to rise and shoot, and then rise very slowly and only enough to clear the back of the decoy.

Do not try decoying during the rifle season, and even when using a decoy during the archery season it's wise to use it only in isolated areas where you know the location of other hunters. Being behind or near a decoy that might draw a shot is very dangerous. Always think about safety before you try any setup with a

Lohman Challenge Call

decoy. If you use a full-bodied decoy, always wrap a piece of blaze-orange cloth around it before carrying it on your shoulder across the prairie.

Because decoying nearly always requires a certain amount of crawling, many bowhunters wear knee and elbow pads for protection against cacti and sharp rocks.

Decoying can also prove effective for those special muzzleloader hunts that take place during the rut period. Again, use a good dose of common sense when relying on a decoy during a muzzleloader hunt. Even the old-fashioned frontloaders have considerably greater range than the best bow and arrow, and some of the more modern muzzleloading rifles can shoot accurately out to over 200 yards. Since the muzzleloading hunter may be able to take a pronghorn from a distance, being right behind the decoy isn't necessary. In fact, a better place to be may be 50 or 60 yards off to one side, away from where the herd buck's attention will be focused.

CALLING

Traditionally, pronghorns have been hunted primarily by the spot-and-stalk technique. This strategy was, and still remains, the most widely used tactic by rifle hunters with the ability to accurately place shots at 200 to 300 yards. However, spotting a good buck and then stalking to within muzzleloader or bow range of the pronghorn generally requires massive amounts of either skill or luck, or both. Most attempts prove to be nothing more than an exercise in futility. But decoying, combined with calling, has greatly improved the chances of pronghorn success with short-range weapons. And while the use of a decoy during the centerfire rifle seasons is ill-advised, calling is a technique that can be safely used to bring antelope closer during any season.

Most wildlife research does not describe the pronghorn as being vocal. The most recognized examples of voice or sound communication are the bleats of fawns and the snorts made by both sexes. More recently though, hunters became aware of a sound bucks make when issuing a challenge during the rut. Through years of observation and personal research, Mel Dutton was one of the first serious pronghorn hunters to identify the sound, which many hunters previously thought was the sound of a bird. The so-called "challenge" call sounds like a raspy snort, followed by a series of "ta-ta-ta-ta-ta" notes. The call and its rhythm are easily learned from buying or renting a pronghorn game-calling instructional tape or video.

The basic pronghorn snort call, without the follow-up chuckle sounds, is believed to be an alarm or warning.

Pronghorn Challenge

A couple of years ago, the suggestion that you could call in an antelope would elicit disbelief, if not the beginning of outright commitment proceedings. Few people believed that antelope used any form of vocalization, and the thought of using calling as a hunting technique was beyond their imagination. This is similar to the general attitude of deer hunters about 20 years ago toward the possibility of using a grunt call for whitetails. We recently learned that an increasing number of deer hunters were buying deer calls to use on antelope. These guys must have been secretive about their technique to avoid ridicule, but they were sometimes making it work.

For years hunters had been hearing strange sounds when pronghorns were near, but most of these folks thought the sounds were some sort of bird call. We started researching pronghorn vocalization and found that they frequently make a sort of barking-snort noise at each other. Furthermore, they make variations in sounds, the most important being the challenge call used during the rut. When comparing my experiences with Mel Dutton, I found that he had been partially successful at calling pronghorns with his mouth. He wasn't exactly great at it, but together we started developing a call that any hunter could use.

Much is yet to be learned about antelope language. Sometimes does come to the call as if drawn in on a rope, then they refuse to leave even when hunters are clearly visible. It isn't foolproof on bucks, but most herd bucks come to answer the challenge or check out the challenger. I have seen some rank bucks come charging headlong towards a call with no decoy in sight from as far as a half-mile away. If you haven't tried calling, do so. You won't be sorry.

- Brad Harris, Lohman Calls

Experts often disagree on how pronghorns rely on the snort, but a single snort call will at times cause a spooked pronghorn to stop and look toward the source of the sound. This should be considered a last-resort hunting tactic, and the hunter must have his rifle ready and be prepared to take the shot. While a spooked pronghorn may stop and look back, it usually doesn't hold a pose for long.

The refinements of decoying and calling have changed the sport of antelope hunting from a strict long-distance game to one that is played out at close range. This is awesome news for anyone who prefers to carry a bow or muzzleloader. The chances for success are excellent for those willing to learn and apply these cutting-edge techniques.

ANIMAL HIDES were sometimes used by Indians to get close to game. The illustration above shows two Indians using coyote hides to approach a herd of buffalo. Because a buffalo's best defense against a coyote is to face it head on and fight,

Unusual Pronghorn Hunting Techniques

There was a time when few deer hunters would admit to attempting to call whitetails within bow range. Now just about every serious bowhunter and many gun deer hunters own and use rattling horns and a grunt call. The same is happening with the newly developed techniques of decoying and calling a pronghorn herd buck to within easy bow range. Today, they're widely accepted as advanced tactics.

Some hunters have never been good at just sitting and waiting for things to happen. Instead, they go out and make things happen, often reverting to extremely aggressive techniques that at first may appear to be quite strange. Pronghorn hunting has certainly not been immune to tactics or techniques that border on the bizarre.

the Indians were successful with this unusual technique. (Detail of painting, "Buffalo Hunt under the Wolf-Skin Mask," 1832-1833 by George Catlin, provided by the Smithsonian American Art Museum, Washington, D.C./Art Resource, NY.)

Over the years, we have experienced a few prong-horn tactics that are, well, unusual to say the least. In the following paragraphs we will share interesting stories that describe our unique tactics.

BURLAP SNEAK – DON OSTER

After spotting the herd of antelope at long range, our stalk had taken a turn for the worse. Using terrain breaks, my son Mark and I had planned an approach to what looked to be a reasonable shooting range. Having crawled and groveled through breaks, cacti and sage,

we topped a final rise only to find that there was a big flat in front of us. The herd was still 500 yards away, on the other side of only sparse grass and stunted sagebrush, offering nothing we could use for cover. There was no way to continue the stalk using conventional sneak or crawl methods, and no terrain break to use to circle the herd. We were stymied.

Left with no viable options, I left Mark there to watch the animals while I worked my way back to our truck to get a roll of camouflaged burlap. As soon as I returned to Mark's hiding place, we both stood up, each holding one end of the burlap in front of our bodies as we walked directly toward the herd. In truth, we felt a bit foolish walking across a wide-open flat toward an animal with such excellent vision. Mark is 6'3"; the burlap is about 5'5" tall. Either his lower legs or top of his head was exposed to the antelope at all times.

As we approached the herd, several of the does looked our way, showing only mild curiosity, then calmly went back to grazing. The herd buck was about 300 yards away, busily trying to round up some does that had wandered away from the main group.

Certain that the buck would settle his problems with the wanderers and bring them back to the main group, we continued across the flat toward the largest bunch of does. We reached a depression within 50 yards of the group and settled down to wait. When the herd buck eventually returned with his errant girlfriends, Mark got into position for the shot, squeezed the trigger, and missed! While he was bummed about the blown opportunity, I was ecstatic that the burlapping technique had worked.

Anyone using the spot-and-stalk technique for pronghorns will be duped many times by the antelope's choice of location and fantastic eyesight. For these reasons, many hunters refuse to believe that "burlapping" works. However, don't write it off until you've tried it. It can work when your stalk options have been exhausted.

Recount the number of times you've spotted a good antelope, planned the best stalk available and crawled to the edge of the last terrain break, only to find that the trophy has moved far beyond your range of confidently making the shot. Some smart old herd bucks set up camp on a large flat where they can see any movement for long distances. They remain with their harem in these safe places throughout the day, using their eyesight as the primary defense against predators or other intrusions. Without the burlap technique, these antelope are virtually unapproachable. Your choices are few; either try an ill-advised shot, wait until the herd moves to where you can continue your stalk, or give up and go find an animal in a location that permits an approach. If you have found an exceptionally good buck where a stalk won't work, what have you got to lose (except your dignity)? Get out the burlap!

Before you move into the open, unroll your camo burlap, hold it up in front of you and walk straight at the herd. You should have the wind in your face at all times. There are mixed opinions among hunters about the sensitivity of the antelope's sense of smell. But it has been my experience that the game is over once they smell you.

The burlap technique works well with two hunters and even better with three. With three hunters, two manage the camouflaged burlap by holding it at each end, placing the shooter in the middle. You may feel foolish doing this until you learn how well it can work. Care must be taken not to stumble over sagebrush, rocks or other obstacles in your path. Coordinate your approach to keep walking shoulder to shoulder in a straight line directly toward the herd.

Most times animals in the herd show some mild interest in the advancing blob of burlap as they occasionally raise their heads and look in your direction. Their tolerance to your approach will amaze anyone witnessing it for the first time. Although you make no pretense of being hidden, the animals apparently don't associate the shape with danger. There's no telling what they think you represent; perhaps they associate the shape with a cow. You know they can see you, but their continued grazing indicates that they are not alarmed.

You want the shooter to reach a distance within his confidence zone. Look for a small clump of bushes or other place where the burlap can be lowered to let the shooter take a solid rest for the shot. At very close range, it may be necessary to take a standing offhand shot over the top of the camo. It's possible to walk to within 50 to 75 yards of a herd as long as the hunters approach into the wind and remain reasonably well-concealed behind the burlap. The technique is very useful to muzzleloader hunters and possibly archers, who must get within very close range for a shot.

I've heard of an alternative to burlapping in which the hunter holds a mirror in front of himself as he approaches the antelope. The theory is that the mirror, held at a slight downward angle, reflects the terrain, showing the weeds, sage and other objects in front of the advancing hunter. From the antelope's perspective, this technique may be barely noticeable as long as the hunter's advance is slow and steady.

THE TROJAN COW – TOBY BRIDGES

For 5 days in a row, the dandy 16-inch Boone-and-Crockett-class pronghorn and his harem of seven does spent the entire day lounging in the dead center of a huge open valley, offering absolutely no way of getting anywhere within 700 or 800 yards of them. It didn't matter if I checked on them at 8 a.m., at noon or just before dark; those goats never moved more than 100 yards from the same spot. And this told me that they were most likely feeding and watering at night.

It was near the end of the second week of season, and I'm sure those antelope had been pressured hard since they inhabited a very wide-open piece of BLM land open to public hunting. But I liked looking at such a magnificent antelope, so drove over to a high ridge at least once a day to glass him.

With only 3 days of season left, a hunting buddy and I decided to drive over late one afternoon and sit there until the sun went down and a very full moon lit up the area. We wanted to see if those goats ever did leave the open valley. And if they did, we were seriously thinking about one of us making our way to within 200 yards of where the antelope hung out all day, digging a pit and spending the night there. I feel it was a plan that may have worked, only we didn't get a chance to try.

We pulled up to my usual glassing point just in time to watch two other hunters pulling something out of the back of another pickup that, at first, I couldn't recognize. Then it dawned on me just what they were doing, and what the contraption sitting on the ground really was. It was a wooden cow. That's right, a wooden cow.

It was actually two identical cow silhouettes that had been cut out of plywood, with several 2x4 cross braces about 36 inches wide connecting the two halves. The silhouettes had been painted up to look like a Hereford steer. When those two hunters stepped inside the arrangement, placed it on their shoulders, then slowly began walking down the slope in the general direction of "our" buck, my hunting partner and I broke out in laughter.

"This I gotta see!" I proclaimed.

There was about another hour of shooting light left, and I just knew we were in for a real show. The wooden cow didn't look all that bad once the hunters had moved several hundred yards off. Then they disappeared into a deep draw, and the next time we saw them they were just beginning to skirt the edge of the flat about 500 yards from the herd. They weren't in any hurry, and stopped for about 5 minutes in one spot. Instead of walking directly at the antelope, the pair slowly worked diagonally toward the animals, then turned and slowly worked diagonally in the other direction, all the time stopping occasionally and inching closer to the pronghorns.

I was amazed that the animals seemed to be paying very little, if any, attention to the lone cow that had appeared from over the hill. And now the skinny-legged bovine had managed to cut the distance to 300 or so yards. That's when my partner and I both realized that as bizarre as the tactic seemed, it was going to work. The smirks disappeared from our faces.

The distance between the hunters and antelope diminished to 250 yards, then 225, and finally at about 200 yards the fake cow turned to face the antelope and settled down to the ground. At that point, the pronghorns were looking at it very suspiciously. A shot rang out, and one fine trophy goat hit the dirt.

When one of the hunters returned for the truck, I drove up to congratulate them on one fine job of duping those antelope. His only comment was, "It works every time!"

Only a few years ago, the methods of decoying and calling were unknown techniques for taking pronghorns. Proponents of these methods were subjected to ridicule and howls of laughter whenever their technique was described. It is understandable why a herd buck would meet the challenge call and appearance of another buck during the rut. But no technique works all of the time. When conditions dictate, you may want to add burlapping to your bag of pronghorn tricks. As for the Trojan Cow, well . . . let's wait and see.

Field-Judging Pronghorns

Exactly what constitutes a trophy animal is a relative and personal thing to the individual hunter. World-renowned big-game hunter and author Robert C. Ruark once commented, "The value of a trophy is computed directly in terms of the personal investment involved in its acquisition." Your trophy doesn't have to be scored, or rank in an official record book, or be listed anywhere except in your mind. A pronghorn buck you've harvested may be your personal best, perhaps big relative to the average-size buck in the location hunted, possibly the reward for your toughest stalk ever, maybe a lasting memory of a high-quality hunting experience or the best shot you've ever made. If you think it's a trophy, record books be damned, then it is!

In the record books, only a few inches of measurement actually separate a good pronghorn buck from a truly exceptional one. Horns measuring 15 inches in length are generally the goal of most trophy-minded antelope hunters. However, a good specimen with main beams longer than 14 inches is generally considered a very good goat. In fact, browse through the pronghorn listings in the Boone and Crockett Club record book of big game and you'll discover that there are about as many 14- and 15-inch-class entries as there are 16-inchers and larger.

The one thing that most trophy-class antelope bucks share in common is that the vast majority of them are 4½ years of age. Throughout most pronghorn range, bucks of that age class are in their prime. Studies have revealed that bucks living to the ripe old age of 5½ or older rarely grow a more impressive set of horns than what they had the previous fall. In most cases, the horns on bucks past their prime are noticeably smaller and often deformed. Today's pronghorn population management techniques, which rely heavily on the hunters' harvest to crop the herds, allow few animals to live longer than prime age. The outstanding trophy heads that are regularly taken from several recognized trophy-producing areas are actually more the product of an exceptional forage base than permitting bucks to reach an older age. Ranches managed for trophy hunting are usually done so by eliminating the harvest of 3½-year-old bucks, concentrating on filling hunters' tags with bucks 4½ or older.

Before submitting a permit application for a well-known antelope area, the true trophy hunter would save time and money by first contacting regional game managers to inquire about the severity of the winter weather and its impact on the antelope inhabiting a specific area. Drought conditions the previous summer and fall could have resulted in animals going into the winter in less-than-optimum condition. If it has been a very harsh winter, there will likely be some die-off. Animals entering a bitter cold, snowy winter need all the nutrition they can scrounge just to survive. Generally speaking, where a summer and fall drought is followed by a tough winter, the horn growth the following year is often substandard. This is especially true when drier-than-normal conditions persist into the following spring and summer. There must be an accessible, quality forage base available for a buck's headgear to reach its potential length and mass.

OFFICIAL SCORING

Pronghorns are officially scored by several organizations. Each recognize a world record and maintain a rank listing of qualifying trophies that score above an established minimum size. These records, along with records for other species and subspecies of big game, are periodically published, normally in book form. The Boone and Crockett Club maintains the record book of big game taken by gun or bow. Trophy animals found dead can also be entered into the B&C Club. The Pope and Young Club keeps records for animals harvested with a bow, and the Longhunter Society is responsible for maintaining records of trophies taken by muzzleloader. All three of these organizations rely on a standardized measuring system, known as the Boone and Crockett scoring system. Safari Club International relies on a slightly modified version of this scoring system and has established categories for modern gun-archery- and muzzleloader-taken big-game trophies.

Using the B&C scoring system, the horns of a pronghorn buck are scored by measuring the lengths of the main beams, the lengths of the prongs, and the circumference of each horn at each quarter starting at the base. Differences in symmetry of each corresponding measurement on each beam result in deductions. The minimum score for a pronghorn to make its way into the B&C book is 82. Pope and Young recognizes all scores above 64, while the minimum score for the Longhunter Society muzzleloader book is 63. The modified Safari Club International scoring system does not make deductions for differences in horn measurements, and has established 70 inches of total horn measurements as their minimum score.

THE RECORD PRONGHORN scored 93⅜ Boone and Crockett points. The scoring form on the opposite page shows the official measurements from the record buck.

250 Station Drive
Missoula, MT 59801
(406) 542-1888

BOONE AND CROCKETT CLUB®
OFFICIAL SCORING SYSTEM FOR NORTH AMERICAN BIG GAME TROPHIES

PRONGHORN

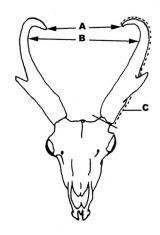
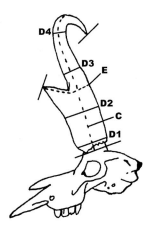

SEE OTHER SIDE FOR INSTRUCTIONS		COLUMN 1	COLUMN 2	COLUMN 3
A. Tip to Tip Spread	8 1/8	Right Horn	Left Horn	Difference
B. Inside Spread of Main Beams	12 5/8			
C. Length of Horn		17 6/8	17 4/8	2/8
D-1. Circumference of Base		6 7/8	7	1/8
D-2. Circumference at First Quarter		6 7/8	7 2/8	3/8
D-3. Circumference at Second Quarter		4 3/8	4 4/8	1/8
D-4. Circumference at Third Quarter		3 1/8	3 2/8	1/8
E. Length of Prong		8	8 2/8	2/8
TOTALS		47	47 6/8	1 2/8

ADD	Column 1	47	Exact Locality Where Killed: Coconino Co., Arizona
	Column 2	47 6/8	Date Killed: 20 Sept 1985 Hunter: Michael J. O'Haco, Jr.
Subtotal		94 6/8	Owner: Michael J. O'Haco, Jr. Telephone #:
SUBTRACT Column 3		1 2/8	Owner's Address:
FINAL SCORE		93 4/8	Guide's Name and Address: Self-guided
			Remarks: (Mention Any Abnormalities or Unique Qualities)

I, _____Walter H. White_____ , certify that I have measured this trophy on ___05/13/1986___
PRINT NAME   MM/DD/YYYY

at ___Nevada State Museum___   ___Las Vegas___   ___NV___
STREET ADDRESS   CITY   STATE/PROVINCE

and that these measurements and data are, to the best of my knowledge and belief, made in accordance with the instructions given.

Witness: ___George Tsukamoto___   Signature: ___Walter H. White___   I.D. Number | W | O | 4 | 4 |
                                              B&C OFFICIAL MEASURER

COPYRIGHT © 2000 BY BOONE AND CROCKETT CLUB®

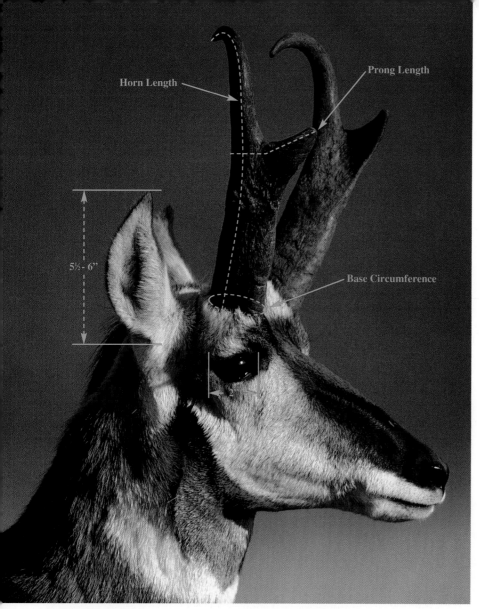

Horn Length

Prong Length

Base Circumference

5½ - 6"

ACCURATE FIELD-JUDGING is really only possible when you get a good long look at a standing buck. You can use the eye diameter of the buck (about 2 inches) to judge horn mass, and the ear length (about 6 inches) to judge horn and prong length. After a bit of practice, you'll be able to field-judge this buck as having horns measuring about 12 inches; prongs, 3 inches; and mass (at the base), 5½ to 6 inches. This young buck will be much larger next year.

Many experienced official record book scorers have a difficult time accurately measuring antelope horns with a tape and square to establish precise measurement points. If it's so difficult for them to determine a score on a table when the horns are in complete control, imagine how difficult it is to accurately judge the record-book potential while those horns are still atop a moving animal in the distance.

Even the most experienced antelope hunters have trouble field-judging trophy animals. First, the horns stand out when compared to the animal's body size, and their black coloration always makes them seem bigger than later measurements will verify. It has

been said that no two sets of horns have exactly the same curvature or shape, making field estimates of the main beam lengths very difficult. Once on the ground, pronghorn bucks have provided the successful hunter with plenty of surprises, both pleasant and not so pleasant, as the measuring tape reveals the truth. Quite often, experienced antelope hunters field-judge a well-above-average-looking buck to be of record book proportions, only to discover that the horns don't even come close to meeting the minimum qualifying score. So called "ground shrinkage" is reasonably common with all big-game animals, but tends to occur more where antelope trophies are concerned. On the other hand, horns that at first may only appear so-so, may end up making the record book. There are plenty of 14-inch horned bucks in the B&C record book. It's sort of reverse ground shrinkage, if you will. Again, keep in mind that only a few inches of measurement separates a good buck from an exceptional buck, and only the measurer's tape may reveal the difference.

Hunters who aspire to place a pronghorn entry in any of the record books must have the dedication, time and patience to inspect, stalk and pass up many good animals until they find one truly exceptional head. The hunter must be prepared to carry home an unused tag if a suitable-sized specimen cannot be taken. In most cases, there will be considerable doubt as to actual size and score even after the shot is made.

Following are a few tips to more accurately rough score pronghorn bucks in the field. These tips should give you some insight to the class of buck you're looking at through your optics.

FIELD-JUDGING TIPS

The most difficult judgment is the length of the main beams, due mostly to extreme variations in their curvature and shape. Bucks with nearly straight horns often appear to be bigger than a buck with very inward- or backward-hooked tips. Begin to determine horn length by comparing the length of the horn to the length of the ears. The average adult

TIME IN THE FIELD is your best training for quick and accurate field-judging. Most of the time a buck doesn't stand broadside and pose waiting for you to size him up. In the above left photo, the buck has great prong length, but the actual measurement is difficult to judge because he's facing you. The buck on the right has great mass and long horns, but you'd better decide quickly to take the shot or he's long gone.

pronghorn buck's ear from base to tip generally measures from around 5½ to 6 inches in length. Provided you are looking at a buck with horns that appear to be 2½ ear-lengths long, you've found a really good buck with horns of around 15 inches. A good cross-check is to establish where the bottom of the prong is in relation to the tip of the ear. If it sits well above and there is as much main beam above the prong as below, you're onto a trophy with real potential.

Judge prongs by ear length. If the prong, measured from the rear of the main beam to the tip, appears to be nearly equal to the length of the ear, you've found a buck with great prongs. Most "book heads" have prong measurements in the 6- to 7-inch range.

The mass or circumference of each base must measure between 6 and 7 inches to add needed points to the score. An antelope's eyeball is approximately 2 inches in diameter. Horn bases that are 1½ eyeballs wide definitely fulfill the mass requirement for the base. The

circumference of the main beam will taper above the prong. However, to score well it should be almost the same size directly below the prong as at the base.

The area from the base of the horn to the tip of a mature buck's nose regularly measures about 8 inches. The measurement can be used to reinforce estimates of both horn and prong length. During your inspection of the buck's headgear, look for abnormalities that affect symmetry of the horns, such as a malformed or short main beam or a missing prong. Measuring systems such as Boone and Crockett aren't very forgiving and penalize a head that is not symmetrical. Differences in measurements from one side to the other of a pronghorn rack results in deductions to the final score. Some hunters highly prize freak horns, but most abnormal antelope horns don't score well. The Boone and Crockett Club does not recognize a separate category for non-typical pronghorns.

RECORD BOOK ENTRIES

Wyoming carries the distinction of being the center of the nation's pronghorn population, and it's home to more antelope than practically all other states combined. It follows that Wyoming leads in total record book entries. However, a close look at the entries reveals that there are prime counties in three states accounting for an inordinate number of book entries. Of nearly 300 entries in a recent edition of the Boone and Crockett Record Book, nearly one third of all listings came from the following counties: Sweetwater, WY; Carbon, WY; Mora, NM; Colfax, NM; and Coconino, AZ. The world-record pronghorn (see accompanying score sheet, p. 109) was taken in Coconino County, Arizona, in 1985, and scored 93⅜ B&C points.

RECORD BOOK BUCKS have long massive horns. In this photo, a hunter is measuring horn length with a ¼-inch-wide flexible steel tape, the same type used by the official scorers of the Boone and Crockett Club.

After the Harvest

Y ou've put in your time scouting for just the right
buck, patterned him perfectly, crawled through
plenty of sticky things to get within reasonable
range, and justified all the time you put in on the
range with a beautiful one-shot kill. Your buck is on
the ground, and as the old saying goes, "Now it's
time to roll up your sleeves and get to work."

Field-dressing and caring for an animal weighing
less than 130 pounds isn't nearly as difficult as caring for game as big as an elk or moose. And a large
whitetail buck, which may weigh twice as much as a
pronghorn, takes much more time and effort to field-
dress, haul out of the field, skin and package for the
freezer. However, most pronghorn seasons take place
during relatively warm weather, making prompt
attention the first step to preserving a nice trophy
and ensuring some fine eating later on. The faster
you get the entrails out, the sooner the cooling
process can begin. As soon as you have your goat
tagged and the obligatory "grip and grin" photos
snapped, it's time to pull out the knife.

Field-dressing an antelope can be as easy or as difficult as you make it. It doesn't take a specialized knife
to get the job done. Any folding-type hunting knife
with a 2½- to 4-inch blade is more than sufficient, provided the edge is sharp. But if you're looking for a
superb knife set, take a look at the dressing and skinning duo available from the manufacturer, Knives of
Alaska. This two-knife set includes a larger knife
(opposite page) with a curved blade and gut hook,
which makes opening the body cavity a snap. The
smaller knife in the set works well for close work
like skinning around the legs.

After removing the entrails, get the animal out of the
field and take it to where it can be skinned fairly
quickly. The hollow hair that does such a great job of
insulating the pronghorn from the bitter cold of winter also does an excellent job of retaining body heat
after the animal has been harvested and field-dressed.
As often as not, the successful hunter can drive relatively close to the downed animal for easy pickup.
But don't always count on it. It's a good idea to pack
along a piece of rope and a harness-type drag strap
that fits over or around your shoulders. Once the
entrails have been removed, a field-dressed buck
may weigh only about 80 pounds and can usually be

pulled along fairly easy. If the buck is destined for the taxidermy shop, be extremely careful to avoid rubbing a bald spot on the cape or breaking off the long, brittle guard hairs. For a trophy mount, the less you have to drag your buck the better.

As soon as feasible, hang and skin the carcass in a shady place. Not only does leaving the hide on for any extended period of time contribute to spoiled meat, it also allows the strong odors of a pronghorn hide to permeate the meat. Also, if the animal is skinned within an hour or so of being harvested, the hide peels off much more easily. And as soon as it's off, remove the windpipe. Normally this is where meat begins to spoil most quickly if the carcass is not properly cooled. Hunters who have found prong-horn venison excellent tablefare won't chance losing it. They usually skin the animal right in the field if there is a tree, windmill, gate post or old building nearby to permit hanging the antelope.

A gambrel and small hoist can make hanging and skinning a breeze. Skin out the back legs far enough to expose the main tendon above each knee, insert the gambrel hooks, tie up the hoist and lift the ani-mal to the desired height for skinning and quarter-ing. A usable gambrel and hoist can cost as little as $20 to $30, and they take up very little room in the back of your pickup or duffel.

As soon as the skinning is finished, take a few min-utes to brush or pick any loose hairs from the meat. Trim and discard any questionable-looking parts, such as blood-shot meat where your bullet impacted. Time permitting, allow the skinned carcass to hang and cool for 1 or 2 days, making sure that it's out of the sun and heat. Within minutes after the skin has been removed, a protective film forms on the outside of the carcass, helping to protect the meat. In warm weather when flies are present, further protect the meat from their invasion by covering the carcass with cheesecloth or a fine-mesh game bag. When it's really hot, finding a cool place to allow the meat to hang isn't always possible. You may have to get it to a meat locker to prevent loss, or quickly bone it out, bag the meat and ice it down in a cooler. If you go the latter route, be sure that your bags are waterproof and try to keep the meat from getting soaked.

A freshly harvested prong-horn is not very difficult to skin. After a few pertinent knife cuts, the skin can literally be peeled from the carcass. How the animal is then quartered,

boned out or further processed depends on the cuts of meat desired. For quartering, a small meat saw or hacksaw can be used to cut off the feet and halve the carcass down the center of the backbone and pelvis. The two halves can then be cut crosswise near the back of the rib cage for four equal portions.

Other hunters opt to fully bone the carcass, rarely cutting a single bone. Using a sharp fish-fillet-type knife, the meat can be easily trimmed from the bones. The backstraps are considered the choicest cuts and are usually the first to be peeled away from the backbone. Generally speaking, a pronghorn can be fully boned in less than 30 minutes.

Every game meat processor can tell stories about big game that was so poorly cared for that it had already spoiled by the time it came through their doors. No matter how it's packaged or prepared, the meat from any game animal that was poorly shot, allowed to lay around for hours before being field-dressed, dragged through the dirt, cooled improperly, exposed to hot sun and heat or otherwise mishandled won't be fit for human consumption. On the other hand, when pride and care is taken to properly dress, skin, cool and butcher the meat, wild-game dishes are hard to beat. The fine-textured meat from a pronghorn is often considered a delicacy.

The head from any buck that is to be mounted requires prompt attention as well. Many taxidermists prefer that the hunter not attempt to fully cape the head. A few wrong cuts and the hide can be ruined. Instead, most taxidermists prefer that a hunter bring in the complete head. However, they often find that even when the complete head is brought to them, the hunter has cut the cape too short. Be sure to include at least 4 or 5 inches of hide behind the front shoulders for the best head-and-shoulder mount. The easiest way to care for a pronghorn that you wish to have mounted is to roll up the entire head and hide, gently place it into a plastic trash bag, and freeze it.

SPECIALTY KNIVES, such as this model from Knives of Alaska, have a curved blade and gut hook for easy field-dressing and skinning.

Pronghorn Recipes

Proper field care is key to having some of the finest pronghorn meat available on your table. Although a dressed pronghorn doesn't yield a lot of meat, the roasts, chops and ground meat make for some memorable meals. Pronghorn is lean and tasty, a good low-fat source of protein. Mix in 5 percent beef or pork fat to give the ground meat some consistency. It will fry up with no grease residue when fully browned. Below are some tasty, easy-to-fix recipes to add to the overall rewards of a successful antelope hunt.

ANTELOPE BACKSTRAP ROAST

Ingredients:

2½-to 3 lb.-piece of trimmed
  backstrap
3 medium onions (sliced)
  salt and pepper
½ pkg dry onion soup mix
½ cup water
1 teaspoon liquid smoke
½ teaspoon Worcestershire
  sauce

Marinade:

Place meat in a baking dish with one crushed garlic clove. Cover meat with 1% milk. Marinate in refrigerator for at least 24 hours.

Preparation:

Preheat oven to 325 degrees. If you use a slow cooker, do not preheat.

Remove meat from marinade and wash thoroughly. Salt and pepper the meat. Fashion a basket of foil wrap in a baking dish or slow-cooker. Line the foil basket bottom and sides with onion slices. Place meat between onion slices, add onion soup mix, water, liquid smoke and Worcestershire sauce. Place remaining onion slices on top of meat and tightly seal the foil basket at the top. Bake in the oven or slow-cooker at 325 degrees for 1½ hours. Test for doneness; meat should be thoroughly cooked.

Drain broth; it can be served over the meat or used as a gravy base. Serve with cooked onion slices on the meat.

ANTELOPE TACO CASSEROLE

Ingredients:

1 lb. ground pronghorn
1 can (16 oz.) refried beans
4 oz. grated cheddar cheese
1 pkg. taco seasoning mix
½ teaspoon ground cumin
8 oz. sour cream
2 medium jalapenos
1 can (11½ oz.) Pillsbury®
  refrigerated cornbread
  twists
2 medium onions (chopped)
4 oz. black olives (sliced)

Preparation:

Brown meat, jalapenos and onions in a 12-inch skillet; add taco mix as meat cooks. Mash cornbread twists on the bottom and sides of an ungreased 10-inch-deep baking dish, forming a layer similar to a pie-crust shell.

Warm refried beans in a saucepan; stir into browned meat mixture. Pour meat-bean mixture onto cornbread shell and smooth to form a base layer.

Blend olives, sour cream and shredded cheddar and add as the top layer of the casserole. Preheat oven to 350 degrees; bake at 350 for 45 minutes.

Serve with salsa and tortilla chips.

PRONGHORN MINUTE STEAKS WITH GRAVY

Ingredients:

8 pieces antelope round steak, approximately 3 inches square and ½ inch thick

salt

pepper

garlic powder

flour

cooking oil

Preparation:

Place meat squares on cutting board. Add salt, pepper and garlic powder to each piece. Coat each piece with flour and pound the flour into meat with a tenderizing mallet. This will thin the meat and tenderize it. Turn the meat, add spices and flour and repeat pounding process.

Coat bottom of 12-inch skillet with oil and fry pieces over medium-high heat until coating is crisp and golden brown.

Milk Gravy:

4 tablespoons cooking oil

2 tablespoons flour

salt

pepper

1½ cups milk

Add oil to frying residue in skillet, heat at medium high. Slowly sprinkle in flour, stirring as flour fries to prevent lumps from forming. Slowly add milk while briskly stirring the mixture. Add salt and pepper and cook at medium high until gravy thickens. Serve over steak or on biscuits.

PRONGHORN GUISADO ↑

Ingredients:

1 lb. ground antelope

4 medium onions (chopped)

2 medium fresh tomatoes (chopped)

1 to 3 jalapeno peppers (finely chopped)

¼ cup water

Spices:

½ teaspoon salt

1 teaspoon chili powder

8 soft flour tortillas

½ teaspoon black pepper

1 can (16 oz.) refried beans

¼ teaspoon cayenne

2 cups shredded cheddar cheese

1½ teaspoons ground cumin

½ teaspoon garlic powder

Garnishes (optional):

salsa and sour cream

Please note: Wimps should cut back on jalapenos and cayenne in this recipe!

Preparation:

Brown the ground antelope in a 12-inch skillet. Add chopped onions, cook over medium-high heat until meat is brown. Stir in water, tomato, jalapenos and spices.

Bring mix to a slow boil, stirring occasionally. Simmer until liquid cooks away, leaving the mixture moist.

Heat beans at medium in a 1-quart saucepan, stirring occasionally. Warm tortillas as directed on the package. To make a burrito, spoon beans and the meat mixture onto the tortilla, sprinkle grated cheddar on top. Fold tortilla and enjoy.

If desired, you may pin the tortilla shut with a toothpick and heat in a microwave for 30 seconds on a high setting. Serve tortillas topped with salsa and sour cream.

Hunts to Remember

Guiding for Pronghorns *by Toby Bridges*

GETTING THE LEAD RIGHT

A teenage hunter and I spent most of a half hour scrutinizing a very good buck. The young hunter was not exactly a trophy hunter; he just wanted to take an antelope a little bigger than the dandy 14-incher his dad had tagged the previous day. I too had filled out the previous day, and while the young man's father guided his wife, I volunteered to take the young sharpshooter to an area I knew to hold several more good bucks. We had set up and glassed for less than 15 minutes before we both focused in on a beautiful buck with horns pushing 15 inches. I could see the gleam in the young hunter's eyes, and knew he would stick with me through thick or thin to get a shot at the buck.

I sized up the situation and the terrain that lay between our position and the small herd of seven or eight antelope. We couldn't have fallen into a better setup. Getting to within 150 yards of the buck and his small harem simply required easing down into a deep wash, where we could walk practically upright and cut the distance to easy shooting range in less than 10 minutes. And that's exactly what we did. However, when we crawled to the top of a slight rise for a look at where we last saw the pronghorns, they were running in our direction – full tilt!

We were hunting on BLM ground, sharing the area with several other groups of hunters. Another pickup had appeared from nowhere, and had chanced moving close enough to the herd to get a shot. Those goats wanted nothing to do with their plans and broke into a full run before they ever got close enough to unleash a shot. And they were bearing down on us rather quickly.

Without any instruction whatsoever, the young man jumped to his feet, and brought the bolt-action .243 Winchester to his shoulder. The antelope were moving at a pretty good clip and almost in single file. It looked like they would pass within 80 yards of where we stood. By the movement of the rifle muzzle, I could tell he had found the buck in the scope and was tracking him.

"Don't forget to lead him!" I shouted.

A second later I noticed the muzzle swing a little faster while he attempted to figure in the lead. The rifle cracked and at the same moment, a big doe right behind the buck flipped head over heels, piling up in a clump of sagebrush. Fortunately, my hunter had both a buck and a bonus antlerless tag in his pocket. Without any hesitation, he flipped open the bolt and chambered another round just as the antelope hit the draw.

The sudden break in the terrain barely slowed the antelope and I was just about to shout instructions for him to double his lead, but the rifle cracked once again. This time the buck rolled like a big cottontail, and my youthful hunter had a trophy that sported horns a full ¾-inch longer than his dad's. To say he was elated would be putting it lightly.

As we admired his nice pronghorn buck, I asked how far he had led the buck for his first shot. He informed me that his crosshairs had been right at the front of its brisket, and when that shot took out the doe right on his heels, the young hunter never needed me to tell him to increase his lead. His crosshairs for the second shot where a full goat-length ahead, and his hit centered the chest cavity.

GETTING DOWN TO BUSINESS

The goal of an outfitter or guide is to show his clients the best-quality hunt possible, ensure that they have a good time, and try like hell to get them shots at the game they came to hunt. Sometimes an entire week is not enough to get it all accomplished. However, sometimes it can be about 6 days more than what's needed.

I had been guiding with Lone Wolf Outfitters (Buffalo, Wyoming) for about 2 weeks, spending one week scouting and one week hunting. My first group of three antelope/deer combination hunters all managed to fill their tags in the first 4 days of a 6-day hunt, then spent their last 2 days in north-central Wyoming enjoying the trout fishing. Fortunately, my next group of three hunters decided to roll in 1½ days early. They drove out from Pennsylvania in a spacious motor home since they wanted to camp near

where they would be hunting rather than make a 50-mile drive each morning.

We located a nice shaded campsite near a beautiful little stream. When they drove into the main camp just before noon the day prior to their scheduled arrival, I decided to go ahead and take them to their campsite. Another guide planned to do some scouting on an adjacent ranch later that afternoon, so I jumped into the motor home with the trio after arranging for the other guide to pick me up in a couple of hours.

As the driver negotiated the huge motor home across a cattle guard, I looked up to see a trio of mule deer bucks standing along a drainage ditch not 300 yards away. Two were very good 25- to 26-inch spread 4x4s. The season was open, and all three hunters had valid deer tags.

"One or two of you might want to look over those two larger bucks; that's about as good as they get in this region," I commented.

With that bit of encouragement, the two hunters sitting at the dining table jumped up, unzipped their rifle cases and crammed several rounds down into the magazines of their bolt-action rifles. We eased out the door, and moved around the rear of the motor home, keeping out of the bucks' sight. The bank created when the ditch had been dug provided all the cover we needed to cut the distance in half. Both hunters crawled to the top, took careful aim and with two shots, which nearly sounded as one, they both filled their deer tags simultaneously. We quickly tagged and field-dressed the deer, and left them to be picked up when the other guide arrived.

As we pulled up to the edge of a creek-bottom hay field, I was surprised to see that it was literally covered with antelope. Four different bands were feeding in the several-hundred-acre field. Two of the bucks were good 14- to 15-inch animals. And as we pulled in next to a big cottonwood tree and began setting up camp, all of the animals slowly moved away from us until all four herds were near the other end of the field, and a ¼-mile-long row of big round hay bales.

"Are those good antelope bucks?" the driver of the motor home asked.

"Darn good!" I answered.

With that, he went inside the motor home and returned a few minutes later with his rifle. He was ready to fill one of his open tags. After a less-than-difficult stalk, we eased up out of the creek cut and moved in behind the row of hay bales. The best of the four bucks was standing less than 100 yards away. At the crack of the shot, the buck folded and all the remaining pronghorns ran for the other end of the field, not more than 150 yards past the motor home. As they were nearly parallel with camp, another shot rang out and pronghorn buck number two was down for the count. Again, we field-dressed the bucks and left them until the other guide arrived.

We finished leveling the motor home and set up an outside cook tent and another for storing gear. The past hour had been a pretty busy one, and as we were sitting there enjoying a cold drink, another entirely different herd of antelope moved into the hay field. The herd buck was a good 14½-incher. When that goat spotted the motor home, he took his five or six does and headed right for the other end of the field, stopping less than 50 yards from the first buck we dropped near the hay bales a half hour earlier.

The remaining antelope hunter looked at me, smiled, and without a word got up and went inside to fetch his rifle. Fifteen minutes later, we eased up behind that row of hay bales; and with one well-placed shot, he dropped his pronghorn buck only 20 yards from the buck already laying in the field.

By the time the other guide did arrive (about 2 hours after we had first driven onto the ranch) five of the six deer and antelope tags were filled. And their hunt wasn't even scheduled to begin yet! The next morning, the remaining deer hunter dropped a nice 5x5 whitetail buck at less than 200 yards, right from camp. Their hunt was actually over before it was ever supposed to start. They spent the rest of the week enjoying some prairie dog shooting, a little sage grouse hunting and trout fishing.

Goat Tales *by Don Oster*

UP CLOSE AND PERSONAL

Even at a distance of nearly a mile, the horns on the buck antelope were obvious standouts. My hunting partner and I were glassing from the top of a butte into a series of ravines leading down a long ridge across a valley. We both took one good look through a spotting scope at the buck feeding with a collection of a dozen does and started planning our stalk immediately. The band was feeding in a small ravine about halfway down the opposite ridge.

The terrain was tailor-made for a good sneak. First, we had to circle to the top of the ridge and find the fence corner we had referenced from our glassing position. Then we could walk halfway down an adjacent ravine in perfect concealment, and sneak up to the edge of the ravine where the pronghorns were feeding for a close, sure shot.

We drove around the drainage to the top of the ridge, progressed over what looked like two washouts from the fence corner and started our descent. Duck soup – go halfway down the ridge, crawl over one more rise, spot the buck, shoot the buck. We walked halfway down, I crawled over the rise, peeked into the washout, and saw no antelope. Had they left? We sneaked through the ravine and crawled over the next rise. The same result – zero pronghorn. By now, I figured that we must have planned the stalk wrong. We couldn't see any antelope down on the flat in the valley, but I thought they had to be somewhere close by. I crawled to the next washout. This washout had a deep cut into the ridge; the near side was very steep, almost vertical. I crawled up to the edge and peeked over. Again I saw no antelope.

Then, in an instant, I noticed a slight movement right in front of me. A doe had taken one step up the steep bank and we were face to face at a distance of about 10 feet. She froze, I froze, and we had a stare-down that seemed like an eternity but probably lasted only about 15 seconds. This stalk had worked too well – face to face was way too close. The herd was spread out feeding along the steep near my side of the ravine, almost within spitting distance. I had either won the stare-down or the doe decided I was up to no good because she launched herself backward off the bank, ran down the wash and took the other members of the herd with her. I shuffled up to one knee and got ready to shoot The pronghorns went down the wash in a short, swift burst of speed. The buck couldn't resist the temptation to stop near the bottom for one look back to see what caused the

ruckus. It was his fatal mistake. After walking 130 paces, I bent down to admire his 14½-inch horns.

ROCKET ANTELOPE

Frank, my rancher buddy, and I looked for two solid days for just one shootable antelope. I figured that they must have been holed up, because even with a considerable amount of effort, we were coming up empty. We covered many miles of territory each day walking, stalking and burning gas in the pickup truck. Finally, on the morning of the third day we glassed a small herd, including a decent buck, about a mile away on the far side of a drainage. Noting their location as best we could and their direction of travel, we planned a stalk to a small wash running down the hillside where we could wait and ambush the buck.

Our route took us up a main draw for a ways, then up one of the ravines intersecting the main draw, leading to our ambush point. Now, you know about "the best laid plans" and how Mr Murphy seems to always interfere by applying his law. It should then come as no surprise that our final crawl up the wash yielded a look at nothing but empty plains.

Now you wonder, did they do their antelope thing and just take off for no reason at all, or did we somehow foil the perfect stalk? We decided to crawl to the next dry wash to get a better look. Frank was on my left as we inched along. Suddenly, he tapped me on the shoulder, pointed to his left and put his fingers in both ears, knowing my .264 was about go boom. I looked to the left and there was the herd on open, level ground like they had just popped out of the earth. I put the crosshairs on the buck's shoulder and touched off the shot.

The bullet struck just as the antelope was bolting, but instead of moving forward, he shot straight up in the air, reaching a height of what seemed to be about 15 feet. When he came down he landed flat on his back. He never knew what hit him. We got up and counted only 78 paces to the animal. As I approached the pronghorn, I couldn't see any horns. A little confused, I looked closer and saw that the horns were completely buried in the dirt. A careful excavation with my knife unearthed two perfect, unbroken horns.

FIGHTING GOATS

Boy – was he a nice buck, horns in the 14-inch class, good mass and a prong that was visible but not gigantic. He must have been some stud, having accumulated about 30 does in his harem. Maybe he was a bit *too* good, because his many honeys certainly attracted the attention of two bachelor bucks that were trying to get in on the act.

Now, this herd buck was one busy guy. His harem was an unmanageable lot, never seeming to stay put or go the direction he wanted. Plus, he had to keep the two hustlers away from his prized harem. They were two smart cookies, doubling up on the old boy by trying to infiltrate the group of does from opposite ends. The herd buck would chase one away, only to find the other one trying to herd some does away from the other side. He would chase the herder away, then return to find the other buck had returned and moved into the herd.

My partner and I watched the harried herd buck charge around several times attending to his management problem as we crawled closer to the does. He was on the move so much that even a long-range shot was not possible, so we watched all the chasing as we moved closer. Finally the two interlopers made a big mistake. They decided the chasing and running around wasn't working out, so shoulder to shoulder they advanced toward the herd buck to challenge him head-on.

This was the big boy's cup of tea. He puffed up, looking as big as a small horse, meeting the advancing challengers with a slow, stiff-legged walk. Neither of the challengers had the size or the will to be a hero. The herd buck was clearly of superior size, both in body and horn. Turned out he was also faster, because when he charged the two and they turned tail to flee, they each were rewarded with a horn-hook in the rump as the herd buck chased them clean out of sight.

We stayed near the does, knowing that as soon as he dispatched the two pests he would return to the herd. Sure enough, a half mile away we saw him trotting back in our direction. After he reached the does, I waited for the first clear broadside shot. My aim was true and the herd buck was mine.

CLASSIC STALK

My son Mark and I spotted a small group of bucks from a ridge. They were roughly a mile away and the only antelope within sight. I couldn't tell, even through the spotting scope, anything about horn sizes. There weren't any better options at the time, so we sneaked into a ravine to go for a closer look.

The bucks were on a flat beyond a small reservoir. Our first few hundred yards up the ravine were easy, we were completely hidden from view. Next, we slid down a bank into a deep gutter cut by water flow to the reservoir. Although the gutter was more than 10 feet deep in places, cows were occasionally using it as a travel route. The trail in the bottom of the gutter was scarcely 2 feet wide with some standing water and deep mud in low spots. I don't know what it is with the soil content in Eastern Montana, but we had to stop frequently to disburse the acre or so of mud clinging to each boot.

The gutter meandered in the general direction of the pronghorns, which were bedded down for a short morning rest. We took turns climbing to the edge of our trough to verify that the bucks were still in place. Finally reaching a point where the gutter led the wrong direction, we crawled out and made like snakes across a sagebrush flat to the edge of a small bank. The goats were still an awfully long way out on the flat. Through my binoculars, I saw one buck that was standing. He had long horns with an exceptionally wide spread.

I told Mark to take a crack at him; we weren't going to get any closer. His shot from the .264 was about 2 feet short. Not knowing where the shot came from, the antelope all stood and milled about nervously. The big guy gave me a broadside pose; I held about a foot over his shoulder and touched off my .300 Win Mag. At the "thwack" report from the bullet hit, the buck collapsed. The 150-grain ballistic tip did its job well. His left horn measured 15 inches; the tip of the right horn was missing more than an inch, probably from fighting with another mature goat.

I know that claims of 500-yard shots by outdoor writers are a dime a dozen, but I counted 445 long steps to the gutter, and another 52 to get to the bank from where we had taken our shots.

I definitely will hunt that area again. I want to find the goat big and mean enough to whip the one I shot.

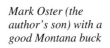

Mark Oster (the author's son) with a good Montana buck

TOUGH PLACES

Everyone knows it doesn't rain much in central New Mexico. Well, my personal little rain cloud hadn't heard that news. Turns out that a hurricane hit the coast in Baja, and the wet backwash from the storm hit during my short pronghorn season. Lightning popped all around my tent during the night, and the wind was relentless. The next morning the winds were still howling at 40 mph, and it was raining heavily. In other words, hunting conditions were miserable. Not only did the elements make the herds as jumpy as possible; some of them went into the toughest cover in the county. Contrary to their normal practice of bedding and feeding where they can see for long distances, a number of herds moved into some extremely thick cedar breaks and hunkered down to ride out the storm.

Here I was in one of the prime big-antelope areas in the country and Murphy's Law had struck with a vengeance. The game turned from the normal long-distance spot-and-stalk process into an experience similar to still-hunting for whitetails in the Midwest.

After several foiled still-hunts through the thick cover, a buck finally abandoned the confines of the trees and offered me a shot. He wasn't a big trophy compared to some I saw on the ranch, but in miserable hunting conditions you sometimes take what you can get.

ONE ON ONE

It's common knowledge among veteran hunters from the West that a pressured antelope buck will run in the middle of a herd of does and hold his head down to avoid identification. I know, I've seen it happen. But during the rut, a wise old herd buck that's been chased and had a few too many bullets kick up dust at his feet will eventually quit hanging around the does and strike out on his own.

Some bucks pick a spot such as a draw or depression to pull off their vanishing act. So when I watch a departing herd from a distance and can't find the buck, I know he's trying to give me the slip. He's probably hiding not far from the herd, so I begin by searching any nearby terrain breaks with thick cover. I keep glassing until I find his hideout, then plan the best stalk to get myself into position for a good shot.

I remember one buck that I thought was pulling the vanishing act, only to find out otherwise. We were making what looked like the perfect stalk on a nice herd buck that had collected a couple dozen does. I hadn't crawled close enough to have risked detection when the buck suddenly left the herd and struck out across the open prairie. I watched him through my binoculars as he trotted off for about a half mile to a little hidden pond.

He walked to the edge of the pond, took a nice long drink, then turned to come back and rejoin his harem. I quickly crawled down a draw that led to a point between him and the rest of the herd and sat down to wait. It didn't take long for the buck to come moseying along past my ambush spot. When he reached within range, he even paused, presenting as easy a shot as can be had on a buck. The .264 barked and the does needed to find a new boyfriend.

It's a fact: a lone buck is usually much easier to stalk or ambush successfully than when he's with all of his lady watchdogs. In my opinion, a one-on-one hunt for a big pronghorn buck is as good as it gets on the prairie.

OVER – UNDER

A friend of mine recently returned from an antelope bowhunt. He was set up in a box blind near the only water hole for miles. The place was comfortable for a long wait and had plenty of shooting ports to cover the entry trails and spots where the goats would drink. It was inevitable that all herds in the area would eventually come in for a drink.

The first shootable pronghorn offered a broadside standing shot. The buck was about 30 yards away, so my friend placed his 30-yard pin on the vitals and released the arrow. The shot went straight over the buck's back. The next shot was also broadside, at an estimated range of 18 yards. This time his arrow went neatly under the vitals, skipping harmlessly into the water hole.

On the second day, exasperation was setting in. He wondered if he'd blown his only two chances. Finally a buck approached, passing so close to one of the ports that all he could see was hair. Thankfully, the buck stopped and offered a very close shot, which he made. The buck was a nice one, but smaller than the two he missed the first day.

My friend's hunt ended with success, but he learned a valuable lesson: Never guess distances on the prairie without a lot of practice. Before sitting in the blind he should have stepped off the distances to all the little rocks and other distinct prairie shapes in his shooting lanes. That way, when a buck appeared he could have checked its position against objects of known distance. He also could have used a laser rangefinder. As a matter of fact, he's been asking about my laser rangefinder. I'm betting he has one of his own before his next western bowhunt.

Index

Creative Publishing international, Inc. offers a variety of how-to books.

For information call or write:
 Creative Publishing international, Inc.
 Subscriber Books
 5900 Green Oak Drive
 Minnetonka, MN 55343
 1-800-328-3895
Or visit us at:
 www.howtobookstore.com

Contributing Photographers (Note: T=Top, C=Center, B=Bottom, L=Left, R=Right, i=Inset)

Robert E. Barber
Arvada, CO
© Robert E. Barber: p. 111TL

Mike Barlow
Livingston, MT
© Mike Barlow: p. 61

Mike Blair
Pratt, KS
© Mike Blair: p. 35B

Toby Bridges
Pearl, IL
© Toby Bridges: pp. 2L, 47, 66, 69, 74T

Denver Bryan
DenverBryan.com
© Denver Bryan: pp. 32-33

Milt Camp, Jr.
Buffalo, Wyoming
© Milt Camp, Jr.: p. 31

Tim Christie
TimChristie.com
© Tim Christie: pp. 35T, 116-117

Bruce Coleman, Inc.
New York, NY
© George Barnett/Bruce Coleman, Inc.: p. 30
© Patricio Robles Gil/Bruce Coleman, Inc.:
 pp. 44-45

Michael H. Francis
Billings, MT
© Michael H. Francis: pp. 6-7, 8-9, 12, 24-25, 29, 36, 42, 84-85

The Green Agency
www.greenagency.net
© Bill Buckley/The Green Agency: p. 112

Donald M. Jones
Troy, MT
© Donald M. Jones: back cover-BR, -CR, pp. 10, 11TR, 14i, 26-27, 34T, 38, 50R, 52-53, 56-57, 80-81, 88-89

Mark Kayser
Pierre, SD
© Mark Kayser: back cover-TL, pp. 71, 78-79, 82, 92, 93, 94-95, 97, 98-99, 100-101, 101B

Lee Kline
Loveland, CO
© Lee Kline: pp. 11L, 11BR, 37, 50L

Bill Lea
Franklin, NC
© Bill Lea: back cover-TR, pp. 40, 48-49

Tom & Pat Leeson
Vancouver, WA
© Tom & Pat Leeson: p. 13

Stephen W. Maas
Wyoming, MN
© Stephen W. Maas: pp. 15, 22-23, 27R, 34B, 41, 49B, 76, 91

Bill McRae
Choteau, MT
© Bill McRae: pp. 4, 111B

Wyman Meinzer
Benjamin, TX
© Wyman Meinzer: cover, p. 111TR

Mark Oster
Seattle, WA
© Mark Oster: p. 121

Kennan Ward
Santa Cruz, CA
© Kennan Ward: pp. 16-17

Art Wolfe
Seattle, WA
© Art Wolfe: pp. 110, 118-119

Gary R. Zahm
Los Banos, CA
© Gary R. Zahm: p. 14

Creative Publishing international is the most complete source of How-To Information for the Outdoorsman

THE COMPLETE HUNTER™ *Series*

- *Advanced Whitetail Hunting*
- *America's Favorite Wild Game Recipes*
- *Bowhunting Equipment & Skills*
- *The Complete Guide to Hunting*
- *Cooking Wild in Kate's Kitchen*
- *Dressing & Cooking Wild Game*
- *Duck Hunting*
- *Elk Hunting*
- *Game Bird Cookery*
- *Mule Deer Hunting*
- *Muzzleloading*
- *Pronghorn Hunting*
- *Upland Game Birds*
- *Venison Cookery*
- *Whitetail Deer*
- *Wild Turkey*

The Freshwater Angler™ *Series*

- *Advanced Bass Fishing*
- *All-Time Favorite Fish Recipes*
- *The Art of Fly Tying*
- *The Art of Freshwater Fishing*
- *Fishing for Catfish*
- *Fishing Rivers & Streams*
- *Fishing Tips & Tricks*
- *Fishing With Artificial Lures*
- *Fishing With Live Bait*
- *Fly Fishing for Trout in Streams*
- *Largemouth Bass*
- *Modern Methods of Ice Fishing*
- *The New Cleaning & Cooking Fish*
- *Northern Pike & Muskie*
- *Panfish*
- *Smallmouth Bass*
- *Successful Walleye Fishing*
- *Trout*

The Complete FLY FISHERMAN™ *Series*

- *Fishing Dry Flies – Surface Presentations for Trout in Streams*
- *Fishing Nymphs, Wet Flies & Streamers – Subsurface Techniques for Trout in Streams*
- *Fly-Fishing Equipment & Skills*
- *Fly-Tying Techniques & Patterns*